NOCTURNALIA

NOCTURNALIA

NATURE IN THE WESTERN NIGHT

CHARLES HOOD AND
JOSÉ GABRIEL MARTÍNEZ-FONSECA

Heyday, Berkeley, California

Library of Congress Cataloging-in-Publication Data

Names: Hood, Charles, 1959- author. | Martínez-Fonsesca, José, author.

Title: Nocturnalia: nature in the western night / Charles Hood and José Gabriel Martinez-Fonseca.

Description: Berkeley, California: Heyday, [2023]

Identifiers: LCCN 2023010089 (print) | LCCN 2023010090 (ebook) | ISBN 9781597146241 (paperback) | ISBN 9781597146258 (epub)

Subjects: LCSH: Nocturnal animals—Southwestern States. | Night-flowering plants—Southwestern States.

Classification: LCC QL755.5 .H663 2023 (print) | LCC QL755.5 (ebook) | DDC 591.5/180979—dc23/eng/20230314

LC record available at https://lccn.loc.gov/2023010089

LC ebook record available at https://lccn.loc.gov/2023010090

Cover Images: Pallid bats, northern mastiff bats, and lesser long-nosed bat photographed by Charles Hood and José Gabriel Martínez-Fonseca
Cover and Interior Design: Debbie Berne

Published by Heyday
P.O. Box 9145, Berkeley, California 94709
(510) 549-3564
heydaybooks.com

Printed in East Peoria, Illinois by Versa Press, Inc.

10 9 8 7 6 5 4 3 2 1

Night is a time of rigor, but also of mercy.
There are truths which one can see only
when it's dark.

—**Isaac Bashevis Singer**

Sunset in Hollywood: in the hills beyond the freeway, raccoons, skunks, coyotes, bats, and owls are getting ready to hunt.

CONTENTS

Sunset comes to Saguaro National Park in Arizona.

1

INTRODUCTION

The desert in the dark is as close as I will ever get to diving in a deep-sea exploration pod. It was underwater back in the Cambrian period after all. —**Neko Case**

What a great, quirky, cool planet we live on! So much to smell, touch, and hear—so many brilliant sunrises, orchestral with the bird world's dawn chorus, and, at the end of day, how grand it is when sunset turns desert saguaros into a dance of shadow and light. And this blue-green marble keeps spinning as we turn off the light and close our eyes, even as more marvels unfurl in the secret corners of the night.

As much as the authors appreciate daylight in all its generous incandescence, we feel that the other half of the clock is too often ignored. Once the sun sets, night can be perceived as a lesser state, one that is deficient, even dangerous. This is especially true in the United States. Over the years, we Americans have allowed ourselves to become alienated from normal darkness. At home we are trained to rely on streetlights and deadbolts, all the better to keep out thieves, insomniacs, werewolves, and wine-addled poets. Even for those of us who camp, urban attitudes often tag along. Some people set up generators and batteries and floodlights, trying to turn night back into day. Doing that deprives them (and their campground neighbors) of the chance to enjoy the very things they left home to experience.

A tongue-in-cheek notice board warns of after-dark threats.

To state the obvious: nature does not stop when the sun sets. In this book, we want to celebrate the other half of life, the unknown half, the surprising half, and what at times might be the scary half. It's normal to be a bit unsure about the dark, especially at first. Please use this book as an opportunity to get past that hesitancy. Doing so is worth it, since so much mystery and joy remains to be discovered. As Henry David Thoreau said, "Night is certainly more novel and less profane than day."

In the following pages, you will encounter glow-in-the-dark flying squirrels, learn about once-in-a-blue-moon blue moons, and meet a dedicated band of rooftop birdwatchers, smartphones ready, who are recording the flight calls of nocturnal migrants. Our invitation for you to join us has several goals. One is to encourage you to contribute to community science projects, the way the birders were doing in documenting urban migration.

More important, going outside at night also provides you a chance to "tune out yet tune in." By that we mean that the usual day for most of us is loud, hectic, and nonstop. Phones ring, doors slam, sirens howl, dogs whine, and on our desk or phone or taped to the front of the fridge, the day's to-do list seems to double in size every four hours. With all that ruckus, it's a wonder any of us can hear ourselves think.

By contrast, nights are almost always calmer, quieter, and (at least in the desert) cooler. The traffic finally has died down; the baby is asleep; the dog chases rabbits in her dreams. What a great time to turn your phone off and go for a walk! You can forget about who is throwing shade at whom on Facebook and finally assess your most valuable treasure: your own self. With eyesight narrowed down to the radius of a flashlight beam, your other senses will wake up and switch on, reminding you of what a complete and well-integrated creature you happen to be.

Can you smell the wet grass, the flowering ceanothus, the new blooms on the evening primrose? Compensating for reduced vision, and no longer being badgered by nonstop urban static, your ears can do what they do best, which is to help build a three-dimensional model of the space you're inhabiting. In fact, if you stop walking (how loud your feet suddenly seem!) and become attuned to the silence, you soon realize that nothing is truly silent, and realize as well how you can hear for blocks and blocks and blocks in all directions.

Your sensory "switched on-ness" goes all the way down to the ground, whether on city streets or country lanes. Even inside shoes, your feet can tell you about the subtle differences between rock and sand, leaves and loam. You walk differently at night: maybe a bit more slowly, even more tentatively, but always more mindfully.

Going out at night expands our understanding of nature. One example of many, but there is a screech owl whose tooting call sounds like a Ping-Pong ball bouncing down the stairs. And even better is a cousin to owls, a night bird called a poorwill. Its cryptic coloration makes it almost invisible—both to us and (it hopes) to any passing bobcats. Sallying from a fence post or dirt road,

A hiker in moonlight contemplates a rushing stream.

José Gabriel photographs a canyon bat during a survey of urban wildlife.

poorwills eat beetles and moths and flying ants. On cold nights, they activate their superpower: the ability to go into a state of self-induced suspended animation, decreasing their oxygen consumption by 90 percent. Coauthor Charles remembers his excitement at seeing one of these desert nightjars in "torpor" in the nature garden of the Natural History Museum in downtown Los Angeles. Nature is indeed all around us—even in the middle of our largest cities.

Twilight: When Our "Day" Begins

As day transitions into evening—and when night pivots back into daylight on the other side—the planet has a magical "shoulder season," twilight. Animals whose activity patterns peak at dusk and dawn are said to be crepuscular, as opposed to those that are more night-adapted (nocturnal) or out-in-daytime (diurnal). There is some fluidity to this; a springtime bear is active more or

This image from 1480 shows how there is moonlight, there is starlight, and then there is angel light.

less all the time, and in winter, you might see a bobcat hunting gophers midday.

In most habitats, dusk is a great time to watch for animals, so we recommend starting your nighttime adventures just as the sun is setting. Sometimes crepuscular behavior is also called vespertine, a fancy word that reminds us that most faiths mark twilight as part of the ritual day. In Islam, the five prayer times traditionally include dawn, midday, late afternoon, dusk or just after sunset, and the evening between sunset and midnight. Medieval Christian practice also divided day and night into units marked by prayer. These "offices" ended with Vespers (sunset, or about 6 p.m.) and Compline (the end of the day, or about 7 p.m.). Modern birders may know the vesper sparrow, so named because of its twilight singing; *compline* comes into the English language via a French word for concluding or completing.

In a more prosaic approach, current legal practice distinguishes three precise states of night's arrival: civil twilight, nautical twilight, and astronomical twilight. All refer to a time after the sun is below an uncloudy, unobscured horizon, and all three apply equally to sunset and sunrise. The difference between the three has to do with the distance of the sun from the horizon (6, 8, and 12 degrees, respectively). The distinctions may seem arbitrary, but they determine such things as when an aircraft must have its warning lights switched on or when the hunting day legally begins.

During civil twilight, you can still see to walk around, but the streetlights will be coming on soon. Nautical twilight means that if you're at sea, the main navigation stars are bright enough now to help fix a position. Astronomical twilight can be hard for city dwellers to differentiate from regular night; car headlights are on by now, and whatever stars you are going to have tonight are "out." (They were there all along, of course, but now you can finally see them.) Yet in a true dark-sky location, during astronomical twilight the faintest nebulae have not yet emerged from the not-quite-fully-dark sky, so the full range of astronomy is not yet feasible. The sky is dark—but will soon get just a bit darker still.

Because of the tilt of the Earth in relation to the sun, the duration of twilight varies by location and season. In cities such as Helsinki or Fairbanks—places closer to the North Pole and farther from the Equator—there are times in late spring when these phases of twilight may last until past midnight.

A monsoon sunset fills the evening sky with a thousand subtle colors.

Tricks and Tools (or the Golden Age of Torches)

Everybody should have a flashlight, both to find their car keys during a power failure and to be ready for a nighttime stroll. In British usage a flashlight is called a torch, a term also used in the wildlife tourism industry in places such as East Africa or Borneo. We'll defer to the American word here, but in the field the authors like to say "torch," since to our ears it sounds as though we're going into caves with our Paleolithic ancestors every time we flick one on.

Headlamps are flashlights that you wear on your head, held in place using elastic straps. We prefer ones with two settings, regular and red light, because a dimmer light attracts fewer insects and protects your night vision. It is prudent to have both a headlamp and a regular flashlight, since there is safety in redundancy. A headlamp frees your hands, so you can still cook dinner, fiddle with your camera, or look in a field guide to figure out which mouse is which. The authors use the same model of headlamp so that we can share batteries as needed, and we usually have a backup light or two or three in our backpacks as well.

A spotlight (and it can be a verb, too: "spotlighting") is a super-duper flashlight that you can use from a moving vehicle. Most night animals have eyes that reflect light, so if you scan a field with a powerful light, you can pick up eyeshine—the glint of a distant animal looking back at you. Spotlights have more power and better "throw" than a typical light, but mostly their names are a matter of convention; there is no absolute cutoff for why one kind of light is named one thing and a slightly larger one the other.

Some rangers and game wardens feel that spotlighting harasses animals, and a mammal enthusiast looking for hognosed skunks was cited recently at Carlsbad Caverns National Park. The actual harm to animals is probably negligible, but wildlife watchers can sometimes be mistaken for snake poachers and out-of-season hunters. Use common sense: never light up houses, oncoming vehicles, police stations, or parked cars where folks are trying to make out.

Luckily for modern nocturnalists, spotlights are smaller and lighter than ever before. Jon Hall has seen more mammals than anybody else in the world, which means he has spent many nights looking for animals in the dark. He remembers trying to spotlight with old-school lighting. You held something the size of a Model T headlight in your hand, and it ran off of a motorcycle battery that you had slung over your aching shoulder. As he says, "Can you imagine walking in the forest all night with a battery like that around your neck? The LED generation has no idea how lucky they are."

José, lit by a bat detector, checks the night sky.

Other night-hike tools you will only need if you really get into the hobby deeply. Extreme mammal watchers use thermal imaging monoculars to help find tree kangaroos in Northern Australia, prehensile-tailed opossums in the Amazon, pygmy hippos in West Africa, and the like. Closer to home, these devices make finding flying squirrels and spotted skunks easier than when you're just using a regular light. They work based on a simple fact: most mammals have a body temperature that is warmer than the ambient air. If you have something that "reads" temperature, you can use it to scan habitat (even a dense tangle of jungle vines) and pick up the heat signature and shape of an interesting critter. You then follow up with a handheld light or a camera with flash.

A bat detector can be helpful. There are different kinds of models; the smallest plugs into the charger port on your smartphone and runs using an app. It makes echolocation calls audible to humans, and translates them into a wave pattern called a sonogram. Some software bundles include identification tips, using a library of prerecorded calls. In the authors' experience, these ID services are a good starting place but are not reliable. We have spent significant time getting to know bats and will talk more about echolocation and bat emergence times in chapter 8.

Last item: a UV flashlight, sometimes called a black light. This is fun to bring because scorpions glow in the dark and are easier to find than with a regular light. We also now know that there are mammals that glow in the dark, including flying squirrels in North America and the platypus in Australia. There may be more than just these—nobody has checked in any systematic way. If you discover a glowing animal, let the rest of us know!

Is It Safe?

What about safety? If you go out at night, will you be attacked by a bear, a puma, a rabid bat, or an evil person? We are pleased to report that in hundreds of hours of night fieldwork and off-trail hiking, a zillion miles of back-road cruising, and 1,001 nights of legal (and sometimes illegal) camping, the authors have come through with nothing worse than two lost flashlights and some mosquito bites. One night in Arizona, we were sure a hailstorm was going to crack the windshield (but it didn't), and in the borderlands, you can expect to have a brief conversation with Border Patrol officers, who may wonder why you're slowly driving a pickup truck back and forth along dirt roads a few miles from the Mexican border. If stopped, have your ID ready and be willing to show some animal pictures from your phone or camera—the Sonoran coral snake (page 88) can be a great ambassador.

Sad to say, when it comes to safety from other people, women need to have a different situational awareness than men, and people of color may encounter extra suspicion and hostility. We asked René Clark, a photographer and snake lover, about her travel experiences. She often goes out alone, and you can see her excellent work in the insect and herp chapters in this book. We asked her, "How do you feel on night excursions—what about going out at night is fun or exciting?"

She wrote back that where she lives, "in Southern Arizona, a lot of animal activity happens at night. Going out, even alone, gives me a great opportunity to photograph spiders, scorpions, snakes, and mammals that I would not normally see active during the day. There is a mixture of excitement, adventure, and fear that makes night excursions exhilarating."

Follow-up question: "Many people are afraid of the dark. How do you manage to be so fearless?" Her reply was quick. "Here is a fact: I am NOT fearless. To be fearless in a wild space at night is reckless. Every sense is heightened, and I am always scanning for danger. When I am out at night, I am constantly 'checking my six' (looking behind me) to keep an eye open for mountain lions, and I am extra aware of my surroundings so I do not inadvertently step on a rattlesnake. I carry a good dose of fear when out at night, which is why I take all proper precautions prior to my outings. To go out at night alone is adding an extra layer of potential personal danger; but the rewards of photographing something that one would never experience during the day are so great, it is worth the risk."

Mary Carmona Freeman, a Los Angeles birder and owl expert, has been another contributor to this book. She has led or organized more than two thousand field trips and eight hundred owl surveys. Asked about safety, she was matter-of-fact. Since she doesn't know how to fix cars, and since you want a buddy along anyway for company and note-taking, she goes with a partner, usually her husband. She is also "very wary of bears and mountain lions—and speeding cars."

Do the police ever stop her? "One night, an officer came by checking on me and my husband. But when he stopped, the first thing I asked was if he had seen any owls. I explained we were listening to owls for a nature survey, and after that, it was fine. In fact, the officer proceeded to describe an owl he had seen, and I gave him ideas what it could have been. It was a fun chat! In the twenty-two years we have been doing owl surveys in Angeles Crest, we have never had any problems with police or wild animals."

A Typical Walk on a Typical Night

So you've gotten a good headlamp and a backup flashlight. You've found a buddy and packed your best field guides. Now, join Charles and José on one of our favorite night hikes, something suitable for kids and newbies and old hands alike, so we can give you a sense of what you might expect when you set off on your own nature adventures.

Our starting point is the Palm Canyon trailhead, Kofa Wildlife Refuge, western Arizona. The refuge name comes from a mine ("King of Arizona"), and the preserve was initially created to protect desert bighorn sheep. They are still here, but so are owls and foxes and many other delightful creatures.

One approaches this "sky island" from a saguaro-studded gravel plain, turning off the paved road and heading east toward the obvious mountain range of red rock. It looks like a fortress of stone, imposing and yet hauntingly beautiful. It is April, late in the afternoon. The immediate landscape is rocky and cholla filled, with the stone face of the mountain rising ahead of us. Waterfall streaks on now-dry cliffs are the fingerprints of a hundred centuries of thunderstorms.

As soon as we get out of the car, we can hear the welcome greeting of a cactus wren—*cha cha chug chug chug*. Wind is from the west, steady enough to lift the sweat away instantly, and it's about 95 degrees Fahrenheit, with 9 percent humidity. As the day darkens toward dusk, space and texture are each more distinct as shadows crenellate the cliffs, delineating each spall and spike.

Kofa Wildlife Refuge was set aside to protect desert bighorn.

Seven o'clock—we have not started hiking yet, but now we see the first canyon bat, and Charles has a bat detector out, a little red box plugged into an iPhone to make the bats' echolocation clicks audible to our dull human ears. More and more bats zip past—the phone lights up with seismograph patterns of transcribed calls.

What are they hunting? A micromoth, the first official bug of the night and maybe what the bats are after too, perches on the tip of a creosote branch. We can hear but not see two distant great horned owls. Crickets: food for the ear, food for night's smallest snakes. And now here is a mystery bat—the detector shrugs, unable to confirm identification, so maybe it's one of the myotis bats, such as cave myotis, a species whose calls are not archived in our ID app.

Technology can bring us closer to nature, if used judiciously; there does not ever need to be a sharp divide between human and nonhuman, or "nature" and the tools that enhance our under-standing of nature. The authors have fancy cameras (probably too many fancy cameras), and we find that a smartphone is a great tool too. So is a good journal and sturdy boots and an insulated canteen. Low tech, high tech, and no tech: it all works together. On a night hike, you get to use all your senses and even extend them a bit—so bring along a bat detector too.

With the bats urging us onward, we get ready to start. It's like being a kid again, doing this hike, since flashlights make anything an adventure. It's just a half mile up to the end of a short trail where you can see the West's only native palm trees (California fan palm, the same species as in Palm Springs). We will walk slowly, looking for everything.

After the silence of waiting, the sound of one's own boots on gravel—SO LOUD. Charles tries to walk slowly, spreading his weight with yoga-smooth steps. It is fully dark now, and the bat detector shows that there is a feeding frenzy overhead. Canyon bats (formerly called pipistrelles) are small and lively, a clas-sic "flitting" bat smaller than some butterflies but more super-charged, more zoomy-zoomy. We catch glimpses just on the edge of the headlamp beams, but mostly they are out of sight up above us, thirty feet or forty feet above the ground.

And now here is something good: down between two boul-ders by a barrel cactus, a harvestman spider, also called daddy longlegs, dances into view. Its white leg spots glow bright in the UV light. We are using regular flashlights, but also one that emits ultraviolet light, the better for finding scorpions. Related to spi-ders, a harvestman is an arachnid with a regular spider body but extra-long legs, as if it were built out of two different sets of parts.

"Look—" José's spotlight has caught some eyeshine.

It is a kit fox, blinking and then melting away, trotting down-canyon to look for pocket mice and kangaroo rats.

The temperature balances on its toes like a ballerina. The air is exactly perfect now: not hot, not cold, not humid, and above all,

Wood rats are large, cute mice that come out at night.

not windy. Still and perfect and silent and arid and exactly, perfectly, RIGHT. It is right for us, as temperate-zone humans, but right for the desert animals too. The day's extreme heat escapes upward in the dry air, and the night brings a cool breath that makes hunting and foraging more energy- and water-efficient. If we feel like moving and exploring, so do animals.

This is a short trail, and at the formal end of it, we can keep going or we can rest. If a family had brought children, this is exactly the kind of place that is a kids' kingdom to explore. One thing we suggest you do with or without kids is to sit in the dark, turn off your lights, and just LISTEN. What can we hear? Our thoughts, our breathing, and the *ribbit-ribbit* of canyon tree frogs.

With lights off comes a chance to use binoculars to see airplanes and stars (and Jupiter and Saturn). José uses a laser pointer to show Charles the constellations. Sirius is the dog star, bright as a planet. Betelgeuse is so red it looks like Mars, but the real Mars is out tonight too, small and orange and dim. There is a smudge that is the Pleiades and a zigzag that is Cassiopeia. Taurus at the horizon, Gemini straight above. Virgo supercluster over the canyon.

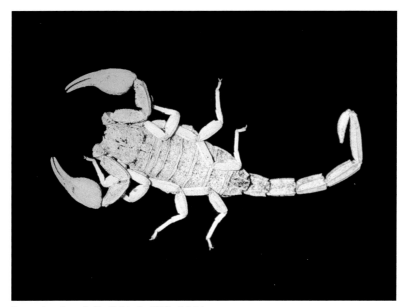

A scorpion glows in the light of a UV flashlight.

After stargazing for a while, José makes a quick circuit with our UV light and finds six scorpions in five minutes, plus some glow-in-dark string and a small millipede, which is a bug-worm with legs, so many legs.

As we walk back we see a wood rat frozen in the spotlight, its still posture saying, "You can't see me!" The wind now blows down-canyon, reversed from earlier. Typically you get valley-to-peak air flow during the day due to temperature differentials, then it inverts at night. At trail's end, a black widow spider ducks under a rock and refuses to be photographed.

What else is around? We jump in the truck and drive down the dirt road we came in on. The tally from a few miles of road surveying includes

- one pocket mouse
- one kangaroo rat
- two kit foxes

- five thousand jackrabbits
- no snakes (we are surprised by this)
- great horned owls again, probably the same ones we heard earlier
- a sky that is dark and enjeweled by stars, but with far-off human presence: over to the northwest is Quartzsite; more south, that must be Yuma; and all along the western edge of the mountains is a borealis of town-glow blurring the horizon, the collective presence of Los Angeles–Las Vegas–all of the twenty-first century.

As a general observation, if you're starting to get serious about nature study, some species—such as ringtails or pumas or the various bats—may all seem a bit mythical. Sure, they're in a field guide, but does anybody ever see them?

The short answer is yes—though with anything, you need to be out looking in the first place. After putting in x amount of field time, the authors now have their "go to" night roost spot for pallid bats, and we've both seen pumas in the wild, and as the photos in this book show, we've also come across ringtails and bobcats and spotted bats. Websites can help (there is a great mammal site where people share location info, www.mammalwatching.com), but it's mostly a matter of spending time in the field. The trick to seeing new wildlife, from skunks to gopher snakes, is going out and looking for it.

Here at Kofa reserve we've had a great night hike (and an equally great road-cruising drive), but now it's time for dinner. We come back to the trailhead and break out camp chairs and a small stove. As we make chicken tacos, one lone shooting star streaks down, reminding us that day or night, outer space never sleeps.

The Night and You

We hope this book inspires action. We often hear that such-and-such topic is the "final frontier." Time to add "nature at night" to the list of the big unknowns. From dragonfly migration to which flowers bloom at night (and who visits them, pollinating), many mysteries and questions remain.

In this book, we'll be sharing stories from average folks who have contributed to community science, and will at times point out areas where your own experiences and observations can extend the conversation. Community-based science, through which small, personal contributions build up to create a larger whole, can add significantly to our understanding of the natural world. We hope you'll be encouraged to join in, using iNaturalist and other resources we will be sharing.

Finally, in night work and in nature more generally, we feel that human imagination spans both the scientific and artistic realms. Take for example this painting of a legacy tree at night. In our view, Georgia O'Keefe got it exactly right when she painted this ponderosa pine in New Mexico. Ponderosas are among the oldest trees in the West, and this was not just any ponderosa but the same tree under which D. H. Lawrence wrote the story "The Woman who Rode Away."

Is O'Keefe painting the tree, or is she painting the night sky beyond the tree? Both, of course, and yet neither: some viewers like this because it looks like a mysterious and powerful squid spreading its tentacles (and its ink) into an infinitely dark sea.

Like night itself, the painting is open to interpretation, and like night itself, it invites us to participate in the making of meaning by sharing our own views and experiences.

Thank you for joining us on this journey to encounter nature after dark in all its mysterious nocturnal ways.

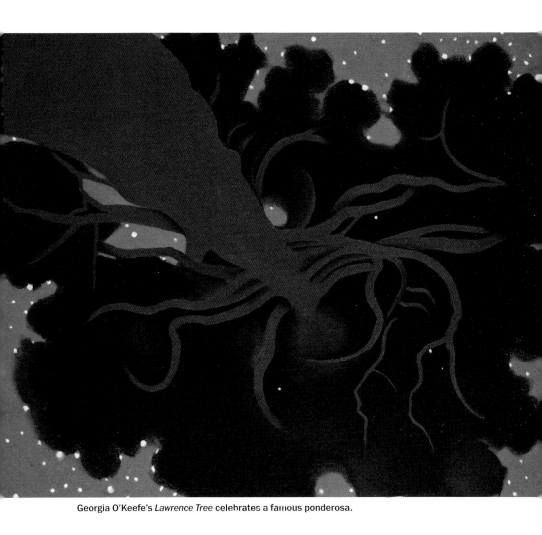
Georgia O'Keefe's *Lawrence Tree* celebrates a famous ponderosa.

Comet Neowise glows bright in the twilight sky above Lake Mead.

2

ASTRONOMY AND
THE NIGHT SKY

The stars we are given. The constellations we make.
—**Rebecca Solnit**

When we look at the night sky, we can usually see a variety of things—perhaps the Moon, perhaps the slow crawl of an airplane, and perhaps (if it's not overcast and you're not in downtown Las Vegas) the light from stars both inside our galaxy and beyond it. Even if it is midnight and overcast, that view still can offer surreal colors and silky textures. And then there are the mega-events, such as the aurora borealis or the Perseid meteor shower. Grand sky or average, there is always something to look at.

In learning the night sky (and in thinking about what "night" means to the animals on Earth), one problem is that to us on Earth, the stars seem part of a one-dimensional tapestry. In actuality, of course, we are seeing many layers of space all at once, and are experiencing local stars but also galaxies so far away they may look like a star, when in fact there are millions of points compressed inside that single dot.

At the same time, it is during the darkest parts of the night that we can see the brightest objects we will ever experience. Unlike our local sun, which is a relatively unexceptional, medium-sized star—what one wag categorized as a "meh"-class object—other stars visible to us are hundreds or even thousands

Many of the photographs in this chapter were taken with basic consumer cameras, not professional telescopes.

of times brighter. For example, Sirius is the brightest star visible to the naked eye. It's about two thousand times the size of the sun, yet looks small since it is just shy of twenty-eight thousand times farther away.

There are more than stars, of course. Depending on how the orbital planes align, some nights we can see four planets besides our own: Venus, Mars, Jupiter, and Saturn. You can see all four of these with the naked eye; they basically look like extra-bright stars, with Venus sometimes called the morning star (and also the evening star), and with Mars being more orange than white. Planets generate almost no light of their own, but instead are giant disco balls, bouncing the sun's energy in new directions, including back to us. (And the Earth itself bounces light onto the Moon's dark face beyond the sliver of a crescent moon, creating what astronomers call earthshine.)

On a clear night, binoculars can help you pick out Jupiter's "Galilean" moons—Io, Callisto, Europa, and Ganymede. They look like tiny white dots next to the brighter pearl of the planet itself. The Galilean moons take their name from Galileo, who

The rotation of the Earth is revealed by this pinwheel of star trails.

first recorded them in 1610. Optics then were new and imperfect; depending on the make of your "bino," your view today may be much better than his original one through a telescope.

And there are a few times a year when all the solar system's planets are visible at once in the same sky, though you definitely will need binoculars or a telescope to make out Uranus and Neptune. And, of course, every night of the year at least one planet will always be visible: the one you're standing on.

It is strange to think about, but all surveys of the night sky involve a "past tense" reality. The speed of light is fast but not instantaneous; whether reflected by the Moon or falling on us directly, sunlight has taken eight minutes to arrive. To look up at night is to be receiving a full dose of "fossil" light: some of it left its point of origin many millions of years ago. In fact, the oldest light we can see right now is coming from thirteen billion years ago, giving us a view back into the earliest days of the universe. And there are many different kinds of light, of course. In addition to visible light, all stars give off light in frequencies we can't see; an infrared map of the Milky Way galaxy would differ in shape and density from an optical-only composite. As dark as space may seem, it is flooded with light—especially when we enhance our own eyesight with telescopes and satellites.

All this light is produced by hot gas made up of familiar elements: hydrogen and helium mostly, but also oxygen, silicon, sulfur, iron, nickel, and neon. Human bodies too are a blend of oxygen and carbon and hydrogen. In the song "Woodstock," when Joni Mitchell sings "We are stardust, we are golden," there is both spiritual and chemical truth in that.

Mr. Bortle's Night Skies

Where will you see the most points of incandescent starshine? In the darkest skies, of course. But how dark is dark? We know that some places such as Sequoia or Death Valley are labeled as "dark-sky parks," but what does that mean, exactly? After all, if you step outside at night, even in a city, it can seem pretty dark out. The quality or "purity" of a night sky—how pristine it is, visually—affects what a human can expect to see when looking up at midnight. The anticipated quality of the night sky can be expressed as a numeric value, using a scale named after the astronomer who proposed it, John Bortle.

This number system presumes a moonless night after the end of astronomical twilight. We met that term in chapter 1; it means pretty dark but not yet *fully* dark, with or without the Moon. Of the three kinds of twilight, all have to end before this scale applies.

The best night skies (the darkest and least contaminated by human-made light) rank as a 1 on the Bortle scale. This is night viewing at its very finest: galaxies are in such clear relief you can make them out without a telescope, and the Milky Way is so dense and granular it seems to cast shadows. (What is the Milky

A crescent moon rises over Turret Arch in Arches National Park.

Way? For more about galaxies, see page 33.) In a class 1 experience, you can even see zodiacal light—a faint glow of diffuse sunlight scattered by interplanetary dust.

In viewing conditions like these, the tired phrase "thousands and thousands of stars" moves from cliché to reality. The sky is so rapturous and densely filled, you feel as though you're falling into it. The class 2 sky is similar, and it's still so dark you can hardly tell what is around you. If there are any clouds, they will just be starless holes in an otherwise rich and varied sky. If you're doing photography, some cameras have a red setting so that you don't lose your night vision messing with the control panel. (A red-filtered headlamp makes a good choice too.)

The scale moves from dark to medium dark to the brightest

and most washed out of all, a sky that is an ignominious class 9 on the Bortle scale. If class 5 is suburbia with hardly any visible Milky Way, by class 9 we are now in the middle of the frenetic, active-all-night, lit-to-the-gills big city. Even on a cloudless night, in a class 9 visual ecology we can only see a very bright planet like Venus, an obvious object like the crescent moon, and a dim scattering of the brightest, most persistent stars. What color *is* a city sky at night, anyway? Sort of a blend of sickly orange and grayish-brown? If there were a Slurpee named "neon lint," it might be that hue.

The good news (or less bad news) is that a class 9 sky can always become a class 8 with simple changes. In the final chapter, we will talk about light pollution and what community members are doing to protect their night skies.

To find those deeply dark class 1s and 2s, head to any of the major national and state parks in the American West: most are highly rated for their dark skies, including the Grand Canyon in Arizona, Death Valley and Anza-Borrego in California, and Canyonlands National Park in Utah. There are online lists and rankings, and even maps to show the relative darkness of each part of the United States. (People don't call the Great Basin "the Big Empty" for nothing.) Idaho has Craters of the Moon National Monument; Texas has the large (and bat-rich) Big Bend National Park. All are designated dark-sky sites.

If your goal is to visit these parks at their very darkest, you need to think about the phases of the Moon and whether there are major forest fires upwind—even if fires are five hundred miles away, that haze can degrade viewing. In Arizona, summer monsoon clouds block the stars. All of these are brief interruptions, and if you have never seen a class 1 or 2 sky, we urge you to make plans to go as soon as you can.

The Moon—Where It Came From (and Where It's Going)

No matter where on Earth you are or how dark the sky is, you can always see Earth's faithful satellite. The Moon is us, meaning it is the Earth, except it is us + them, and in this case the "them" was a rogue planet that careened into Earth 4.5 billion years ago and whacked off a divot the size of Australia. The debris fields from that collision coalesced into a planetoid larger than Pluto, which in time became the sister-buddy we now call the Moon. (Astronomers use a capital *M* when they mean the specific named object, "the" Moon. Other planets and planetoids have moons too, lowercase—over two hundred moons total in our solar system.)

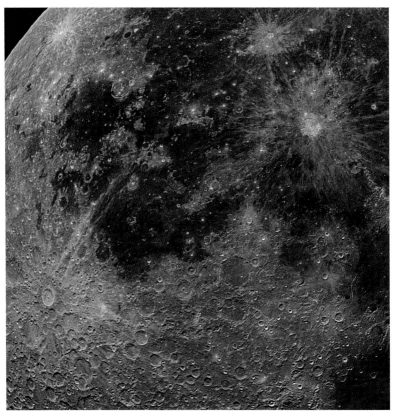

On a calm night, a telephoto lens captures the Moon's surface in fabulous detail. You can also see this view by looking through a birder's spotting scope.

Structurally the Moon is a composite of Earth rock and hit-and-run rogue-planet rock, plus new deposits smashed into the surface by millions of meteors and comets. These special-delivery visits brought new chemicals to the Moon but also fresh water, stored now as ice in the perpetual shadows of polar craters, where temperatures drop as low as −400 degrees Fahrenheit. Will that ice help people live on the Moon? Some futurists hope so.

What looked like seas to the ancients we now know are the shimmering remains of vast lava flows. These are "fossil" flows; there are no active volcanoes on the Moon today. With binoculars or a birder's spotting scope, when the Moon is about at a quarter full, you can make out an amazing amount of topography right at the sun/shadow boundary—crater rims and mountain edges that look sharp enough to cut a finger on.

What will happen to the Moon in the long run? It won't ever crash into us; it is in a stable orbit, and in fact moves away from us about an inch a year. No, both the Earth and Moon face the same inevitable fate: in just under eight billion years, as the sun senesces and becomes a red giant, it will swell past its normal size. As it does so, it will engulf everything from Mercury to a boundary point between the Earth and Mars, swallowing the inner planets—what for the Earth will be the ultimate version of global warming.

Lunar Phases

When the Moon is fully lit by the sun, we call it a full moon; when the Moon is between us and the sun, it looks all-dark, or new. A crescent moon is in between the two. In actuality, the Moon is always half lit and half dark (just as Earth is); we just don't see it that way from our planet-bound perspective. If we could step back far enough, we would appreciate that whatever phase we're seeing on Earth, the opposite phase is happening on the far side of the Moon. And while we only ever see one terminator (the name given to the dividing line between the light and dark parts of the lunar surface), there are actually two of them circumnavigating the Moon exactly 180 degrees apart. There is the morning terminator (which ushers in the lunar day) and the evening terminator (which brings the night behind it).

From Earth we always see the same side. The Moon is locked into our orbit in such a way that there is indeed a "dark" side (though it gets sunlight)—dark in this sense means unknown or unobserved. We always see the same side because the Moon rotates once on its axis in exactly the same time it takes to orbit Earth, which is twenty-seven days and seven hours. There is a bit of wobble, though; collectively, over the course of a year, we see a bit more than 50 percent of the Moon, once all the deviations are factored in.

"Once in a blue moon" means something rare or strange. The expression comes from a farmer's almanac and originally referred to two full moons in the same month.

Animals and the Moon

Among birders and mammal spotters there's an often-repeated piece of lore that it is harder to see owls and kangaroo rats and such during nights when there a full moon, since they avoid bright conditions. The rodents don't want to be eaten by kit foxes and hence are less active when it's bright out. Ditto small owls, which are predated by larger ones. This is sometimes called lunar phobia. Johan Eklöf in *The Darkness Manifesto* explains that "under a brightly shining moon, toads and frogs don't sing as loudly, and salamanders, beetles, and moths forgo their nocturnal escapades." That makes it sound as though they stop going to masked balls or give up playing ding-dong ditch. What Eklöf is trying to document, though, are the data that prove or disprove the lore,

Badgers may be more active on moonless nights.

and to show that darker nights may be safer than brighter ones, and so more animals are out once the Moon has set and on cloudy nights, or on the nights of a new moon.

Of course we can invert that reasoning and say that predators are visible in moonlight as well, and thus a brightly lit night might be better for a mouse-sized animal, since it can see danger before it pounces. And for some animals, moonlight is a navigation aid.

Switching to the hunters, not the hunted, abundant moonlight could be a good thing, as it is for black swifts. These are birds that nest behind waterfalls or along sea cliffs and are aerial bug snatchers: they do everything "on the wing," from feeding to mating. Black swifts from North America migrate to the Amazon Basin during the northern winter. Tracking data on these migrant swifts shows that on nights of a bright Moon they rise up to a higher altitude than usual, presumably to make use of better hunting conditions. The study period included a total lunar eclipse, during which they dropped down immediately to treetop height. When the moonlight returned, they ascended again. Do swifts like the full moon? Apparently so.

In a survey done in Arizona, badgers hunted more actively on nights of a new moon, presumably because their prey base was more active. Want to know how things work in your particular neighborhood? Science does too: set up a study route and let your local biologists and naturalists know what you find out.

Galaxies (Including the Milky Way)

After moonset, when the sky is darkest, both neighboring and far-distant stars will be more apparent. Our solar system is part of the Milky Way galaxy, a flat spiral of around 300 billion stars that is 400,000 light-years across but only 1,000 light-years thick. The name of our galaxy comes from the milky glowing strip of sky caused by the billions of stars and dust clouds, all of it too far away to resolve individually with our eyes. In fact, the Latin name for the galaxy is *via lacteal*, and even the word *galaxy* means "milky circle" in ancient Greek.

For a long time, the Milky Way was assumed to be the entire universe. We now know that the Milky Way is one of at least 100 billion galaxies. Using the Mount Wilson Observatory in Southern California, Edwin Hubble proved that many objects previously thought to be clouds of dust and gas were actually galaxies beyond the Milky Way. All these galaxies form their own neighborhood clusters. The Milky Way, the Andromeda Galaxy, and the Triangulum Galaxy, together with a few dozen dwarf galaxies, form what is known as the "Local Group," which is to say, a coalition of our most immediate celestial neighbors. That is a lot of stars, yet the Local Group is just part of bigger group of over one hundred thousand galaxies called the Laniakea Supercluster.

Thanks to Hubble's research and that of others later, we now know that the night sky is more densely populated than any previous estimates had prepared us for. How many stars? *So many stars.*

This photo of the Orion Nebula was taken in Charles's backyard, an hour east of Los Angeles. To compensate for light pollution, this shot layers forty photographs one on top of the other.

You can see details of other galaxies with binoculars. With assistance from a phone app or a well-informed friend named José, if you get out of the city you should be able to find the Orion Nebula, the Andromeda Galaxy, and the Pleiades, a gorgeous cluster of new stars and blue gas and dust. And of course, dark, clear skies are best for all stargazing explorations. In the Northern Hemisphere, our own Milky Way is best seen on moonless nights in midsummer; you can also review online moon charts to avoid being disappointed by a sky that will be washed out when the Moon rises.

To get the best photographs of the Milky Way, use a tripod to keep the camera steady, and set your camera to a fifteen-second exposure. If you don't have a cable release (to trip the shutter without jiggling the camera), try using the self-portrait timer. If you don't have a tripod, organize your settings and then put the camera on the ground, pointing up. You can use a folded sweater

A close-up of the center of the Milky Way.

to point it in the right direction. Even your smartphone can take good photos.

While summer is classic Milky Way time, spring is known by astronomers as the "galaxy season" because in the Northern Hemisphere, spring is the time when the Earth's tilt points away from the Milky Way's disk, allowing better views of out-of-the-galaxy objects. Winter can be cold but clear and has its own calendar highlights, such as the Geminids, a meteor shower we will investigate in a few pages.

Messier Objects

In 1774, French comet-hunter Charles Messier published a list of fuzzy objects in the night sky, hoping to prevent people from mistaking them as comets. This list of not-comets ended up becoming his most famous work.

The 110 sky features now known as Messier objects are each delineated by a letter and number. M1 is the Crab Nebula, and M16 is the Eagle Nebula; the Pleiades are M45, and the Orion Nebula is M42. Most can be seen with binoculars, and many amateur astronomers "collect" Messier objects the way birders chase rare birds. These bright, interesting, and even colorful sky features can be found throughout the year—for example, the Pleiades are at their best in January.

Don't have binoculars or want to use a good telescope? See the section on "star parties," page 42.

Commonly called the Pleiades or Seven Sisters, M45 is known as an open star cluster.
It contains over a thousand stars.

Noctilucent Clouds

Back within our own atmosphere are other skyborne phenomena you can only see at night. Noctilucent (or "night shining") clouds are thin, ethereal, cirrus-like clouds that can only be detected during astronomical twilight, when the land below is in shadow and only the highest, smallest particles are still catching the sun. As evening falls, they glow a pearly white-blue, high up in the night sky—ghost ice, space hiss, wraith breath. They occur only in the mesosphere, which is basically a frigid band of ultradry air nine times higher than Mount Everest. They are the highest clouds on Earth, forming many times higher than a normal plane can fly. Some data sets suggest that the phenomenon is becoming more common, perhaps due to increased methane in the atmosphere.

A look-alike sky feature appears after rocket launches, such as the one shown here, photographed in Charles's backyard in the California desert. Water vapor in the exhaust plume has frozen and then been swirled back and forth by high-altitude winds, so no, the rocket was not off course, nor was it being ridden by Elon Musk waving a cowboy hat like Major Kong in *Dr. Strangelove*.

Noctilucent clouds occur in the Southern Hemisphere too, but are reported less often. Fewer people there to see them, or just different conditions? Nobody is quite sure. Add that to your long list of "things we wish we knew more about."

ISS—the International Space Station

Riding higher than the clouds but still within Earth's atmosphere at three hundred miles up, the International Space Station is flying past at seventeen thousand miles an hour. It achieves that velocity despite being an awkward conglomeration of pipes, tubes, and solar panels that looks more like an abandoned oil refinery than it does the starship *Enterprise*.

Noctilucent clouds over Laboe, Germany.

Cloud, UFO, or rocket launch? (Rocket launch.)

You can see the ISS on a clear night, with binoculars optional. A dark sky is best, as you would expect, and you should let your eyes adjust if you've been inside or driving. The ISS rises in the west and looks like a bright star, and it moves so fast that a telescope would have a hard time keeping up. Not all nights are optimal; the best viewing conditions are on moonless nights and when the ISS will be directly overhead at your location.

To find out when that will be, NASA has a satellite prediction website. Another good site is called Heavens Above, which also has a phone app version. To start, it will want to know where you are; either select from the list or use the global map. It can generate a sky chart for your location, so you can see not only the ISS but all the other shining glory as well.

What Comes Next

The more we learn about the sky, the stranger and more marvelous the universe becomes. We end with a playful poster from NASA, mock-advertising a space holiday to PSO J318.5-22, a rogue planet with no home star.

Jazz musicians and astronomy buffs, take note: on this world, it would be night perpetually.

Getting More Involved—The Perseids and Other Meteor Showers

The Perseids, Geminids, Leonids, and Lyrids: these are some of the recurring meteor showers that fill out a skywatcher's calendar. Although there are always random meteors—what are often called shooting stars—entering the atmosphere, certain times of year promise a very special kind of show. A meteor shower occurs when the Earth passes through the tail of a comet or when there is some other precipitating cause, and many meteors per hour shoot down out of the sky from one originating point, called the radiant. As the dust particles heat up in the atmosphere, they incinerate in a white-hot blaze. Larger boulders become fireballs, bright as fireworks. During the best, most intense displays, so many meteors flare out at once that it can be hard to count them all. A meteor that makes it through the superheated air to land on the surface becomes a new kind of object, a meteorite.

A whimsical NASA poster advertises tours to a rogue planet where it is always night.

Getting More Involved—Star Parties (Beginners Welcome!)

One of the best options for enthusiasts and beginners alike is to visit a public observatory or to attend a star party hosted by an astronomy club or university. Many state and national parks also offer stargazing activities.

Star parties are like massive picnics, only with camping and telescopes. Often they attract dozens or even hundreds of attendees, many of whom bring their own telescopes and almost all of whom want to help beginners get started. Websites such as skyandtelescope.org and the events pages of the International Dark-Sky Association (page 202) have lists of many of the star parties in the United States and Canada, but always check with your local astronomy group to see about more intimate, local options.

If you see somebody in your campground unloading a telescope (or unpacking a suspiciously sturdy tripod), introduce yourself and ask whether they are going to be doing any observing that evening, and if so, would they mind if you tag along.

A ranger uses a laser pointer during a star festival at
Theodore Roosevelt National Park, North Dakota.

Inside a datura blossom, a spider inspects a lucky catch.

3

DO PLANTS SLEEP?
BOTANY BY MOONLIGHT

Leaves are verbs that conjugate the seasons.
—**Gretel Ehrlich**

Nature thrives using the barter system. You give me some calcium, and I'll give you some bones and antlers. You give me some sunlight, and I'll give you an ear of corn. In old primary school charts, this was shown as a pyramid—plants on the bottom, leading up to a puma or bald eagle at the top. (Whenever there is a shark or a pack of wolves in a nature example, it always seems as though they're a proxy for a human, since we know in our deepest hearts that if there is such a thing as an apex animal, it has to be us.)

Although a better shape than a pyramid might be a honeycomb or tangle of yarn or even overlapping Venn diagrams, it is true that plants outnumber pumas, and just as we learned in school, it is also true that (almost) all plants, algae, and cyanobacteria perform photosynthesis. To do their alchemy, plants start by taking in carbon dioxide and water from the air and soil. Within the plant's cells, the water is oxidized, meaning that it loses electrons, while the carbon dioxide is reduced, meaning that it gains electrons. This transforms the water into oxygen and the carbon dioxide into glucose. The plant then releases the oxygen back into the air and stores energy within the glucose molecules.

The creosote in this view is not static; branches swell and move at night.

This process helps create and maintain the oxygen content of the atmosphere.

After dark, even though there's no sunshine and hence no direct photosynthesis, plants still have work to do. Botanist Peter Thomas points out that "trees and other plants are not dormant or 'asleep' in the cool of the night. Trees do most of their growing at night, perhaps because water stress is lower." Coastal redwoods are moving water around in significant ways, and have the stomata (gas valves) open in their leaves, perhaps to help pull water to the topmost layers and also because nighttime fog condenses on the needles and enters the system from the top down, rather than roots-up as it is in most water circulation systems.

So much is going on that a plant's shape changes. Scanning with lasers shows that many plants bend and pulse at night. In the case of one magnolia tree, measurements revealed that there was a cycle of movement three times a night, with each cycle taking about four hours. As water circulates in plants, the branches stiffen and swell, and in a study of desert creosote, on a windless night even dead branches changed position, presumably due to small changes in the humidity of the air. In the morning, some plants reset their branches back to their original positions and others didn't, ending up "caught in the act" by the laser surveys.

Plant Clocks: How Do They Know What Time It Is?

Light can be measured by both its intensity and its hue, meaning how strong and blue it is (which implies stark noon light) or how soft and amber (the "golden hour," beloved by cinematographers). All living creatures have genetic coding that creates a circadian rhythm, and that "on/off switch" is tied to our perceptions of the quality of light. We "know" what (and hence when) sunset is, subconsciously and continually. That is why computer screens at bedtime are so toxic to good rest, and why artists like Thomas

Hooker's evening primrose is pollinated by crepuscular bees and nocturnal moths.

Kinkade know that painting a tidy cottage with a golden, firelit glow in the windows creates a sense of comfort.

In plants, the light sensors are called phytochromes, and those structures are also found in bacteria and fungi, and even in single-celled prokaryotes. Phytochromes regulate the germination of seeds, the synthesis of chlorophyll, the elongation of seedlings, and the timing of when a mature plant produces flowers. They work in concert with sugars inside the plant to track time and tell the plant when it is appropriate to start photosynthesizing. In one recent experiment, researchers manipulating the sugars in a lab caused the plants' clocks to become misaligned by several hours a day. (If you've ever had jet lag, you may know how they felt.)

As plants "wake up" in the morning and respond to sunrise, the collective change in their rate of transpiration is visible from space. Sensors mounted on the International Space Station use a radiometer to measure the thermal infrared energy emitted by plants. These data can be used to create color-coded maps, and as the morning progresses, the maps show vegetation responding to daylight from east to west, like a giant carpet being unrolled across New England and the Great Lakes. These plants have had a busy night and, through the magic of photosynthesis, will be fueling up for the days and nights ahead.

Pollination after Dark

It is not enough to grow and look pretty; plants also need to be pollinated for the health and genetic diversity of their seeds. Some use wind to achieve this, some use hummingbirds, some use bees and other insects, and some use all the tools of the night. Flowers that open at night are often white and showy—in dim light, this is not the time to be subtle—and usually offer strong olfactory clues as well.

Most night-blooming flowers are pollinated by moths. In the West, plants that have evolved to solicit nocturnal pollination include evening primrose, golden columbine, rock trumpet, ajo lily, the four o'clocks, and the evening-blooming morning glories. Datura is another night bloomer and common roadside plant. It has white, trumpet-shaped blossoms. You probably have seen it, since it can stay open during the day and grows easily and prolifically in dirt lots and along the margins of rural roads. You can see the flowers even if you're going sixty miles an hour. Their intended audience is not us but moths, such as the white-lined sphinx moth. Many monkey flower species are also pollinated by this moth.

above: Datura can stay open during the day, but is primarily a night-blooming plant. It is also called jimson-weed or locoweed.

left: Golden colum-bine seems to be part orchid, part party favor.

Finding a sphinx moth caterpillar tells us that spring has arrived in the desert.

The white-lined sphinx moth hovers like a hummingbird and can be mistaken for one, as well as for a butterfly.

Moths and Bees

Moths come in many colors and shapes, and there are at least fourteen thousand species worldwide. Like daytime's humming-birds, moths come to night flowers for the nectar and only sec-ondarily do the plant the service of moving pollen from plant to plant.

Small and overlooked as they may be, moths and other insects help make the landscape of the American West possible. For instance, Joshua trees are pollinated by yucca moths, which raise their young on the plant's seeds; tree and insect are com-pletely reliant on each other. Moths ignore political boundaries; migrating moths cross the border as freely as the air itself. Why

Desert globemallow has apricot-orange flowers. One kind of solitary bee likes to spend the night inside its closed blossoms.

are there so many moth-attracting plants in our dry Southwest? According to hawkmoth experts Robert Raguso and Mark Willis, "Moth pollination is more prevalent in the Southwest due to warm evenings, favorable climate, and proximity to the moth-rich canyons and thornscrub of northern Mexico."

The hawkmoths or sphinx moths (the names are interchangeable) are about four inches by four inches and famously have a foot-long tongue. That is a large insect, one easily watched with a pair of birding binoculars.

Other flower–insect interactions do not involve pollination. The desert globemallow is a sage-green plant with papery orange blossoms about the size of your pinky nail. The globe mallow bee does not return to a communal hive at night. Instead, it has a clever trick for sleeping. Just before sunset, the bee crawls inside a globemallow flower and waits. As the plant closes its blossoms for the night, the bee gets trapped inside and now has a warm, one-bee tent, inside of which it can rest until dawn.

Queen of the Night

One night-flowering cactus blooms so rarely that when it does have flowers, it becomes the instant hit of the desert botanical season. Queen of the night cactus, also called the night-blooming cereus, is native to Texas, Arizona, and northern Mexico. It produces a fragrant white flower, usually in early summer. On average, the flower survives for only one night—if you hear that it is starting to bloom, drop everything and come see.

The queen of the night cactus blooms only one night a year.

The main stem looks like a dead thorn branch, at least above ground. Under the surface is the main energy reserve: a brown tuber shaped like a human tooth and as big around as a bowling ball. It can weigh up to fifteen pounds. All the queens in an area will bloom on the same night, hoping to attract hawkmoths. Later in summer, this cactus produces a red fruit, which is how the seeds are distributed for a new plant to start up. Few people pay attention to that—it is the blossom that gives the plant its fame.

The Tohono Chul Garden in Tucson maintains a collection of these cacti. A docent, Betty Carras, remembers what it was like in early days, before the bloom became famous. She says, "Watching carefully, we could actually see the opening spurts of the blossoms. Slowly but inexorably the bud became a flower. Ghostly white, it gradually opened its funnel-shaped blossom—becoming more aromatic as it increased in size. By the time its slender white petals were almost fully opened and the flower nearly five inches across, it was extremely fragrant. The velvet-like embrace of warm night air, the magic of a sweet-scented evening, and the distant chorus of singing coyotes made it truly a night to remember."

Bats and Cacti, Cacti and Bats

Many borderland cacti and agaves use bats as pollinators. We will look at bats as a group starting on page 145, and while most bats worldwide use echolocation to hunt flying insects, many bats are nectar eaters or fruit gatherers, especially in the tropics.

Three nectar bats regularly come to the United States. Two are mostly in Arizona—the lesser long-nosed bat and the Mexican long-tongued bat—and one is mostly in Texas around Big Bend National Park, the greater long-nosed bat. Saguaros need Arizona's bats; their pollination depends on it. These species also pollinate cardon and organ pipe cacti, as well as several

A gibbous moon rises behind saguaro blossoms. Calling all bats!

Researchers caught this bat in a net. Its fur is yellow with pollen.

agave species. They migrate here from as far away as Jalisco, and some have learned how to raid backyard hummingbird feeders. Since these bats can live up to twenty years, one yard may be being "robbed" by the same bat year after year.

To slurp up nectar, a bat's tongue has bumps along the side like a sponge or a pipe cleaner. All of this is quick as a flash: the tongue goes in and out of the flower (or hummingbird feeder) in about .40 of a second. The bat makes a swooping approach, but can't really hover very well, so it brakes to a stall, takes a quick hit of sugar juice, and peels away like a jet leaving a dogfight. As they visit flowers and feeders, they can fly upright, sideways, and even upside down.

When not pollinating, bats still help, especially later in the season. They will eat the ripe saguaro *tuna* or fruit, distributing the cactus seeds via their guano. They are very good at this, in

In and out—the raider grabs nectar at a feeder and leaves.

part because they cover a lot of ground; radio tracking shows nectar bats in the American deserts covering a hundred miles per night.

We know that hummingbirds are the classic nectar drinkers, yet all hummingbirds are also insectivorous. They cannot survive on sugar alone, so to create a balanced diet, they supplement flower visits with sallying after insects. By contrast, nectar bats' snouts are long yet weak, and to save weight, these bats have given up most of their teeth. Flycatching the way a hummingbird does simply can't happen. Instead, nectar bats use their long, flexible tongues to collect the pollen grains that accumulate on their fur, licking their way to good health. Hummingbirds can't do this—their beaks and tongues don't bend that way—nor can hummingbirds digest pollen. Nectar bats can (and do) digest pollen, and in fact, it is an important nutrient source for them.

For bats, a blooming saguaro does indeed provide "one-stop shopping."

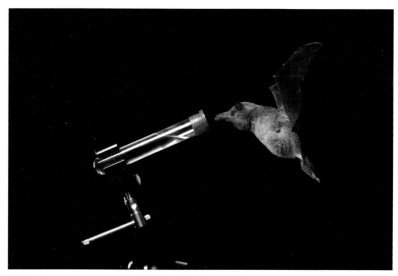

A bat makes an approach to a test tube full of sugar water.

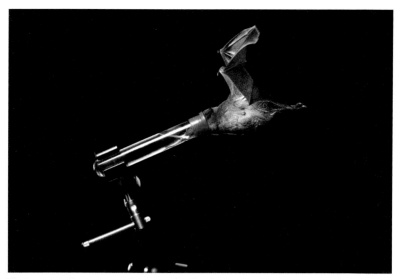

The tongue soaks up nectar almost too fast for the camera to catch.

Getting More Involved—Designing a Moon Garden

Moon gardens do what regular gardens do, but with the intention that they will be enjoyed after dark. That means the designers blend light-colored and fragrant night-blooming plants, sometimes with an audio component (water, chimes), and sometimes in a small space—you could create one on an apartment balcony or in a part of the yard viewed from a kitchen window. Street lights are the enemy here; the idea is to let moonlight itself fill the space with light. A bench is good, or fairy lights, or plants with silvery foliage. To know which garden plants create good moth habitat, search online for a pdf by Meghan Ashley Peterman titled "California Native Moon Garden Plant List."

Why did the tarantula cross the road? We don't know,
but move it to safety if you see one trying.

4

COOL, NOT CREEPY
ARACHNIDS, INSECTS, AND ONE FAIRY SHRIMP

Either the Darkness alters—
Or something in the night
Adjusts itself to Midnight—
And life steps almost straight.
—**Emily Dickinson**

Here's a way to make any summer party more successful. You need a UV lightbulb, a white sheet or drop cloth, a hank of utility line or an old tent pole, and a battery or extension cord to run the light. Hang the light outside as high as you can, turn it on after dark, and use the drop cloth as a backing sheet so you can see what arrives. Leave a bit as a skirt at the bottom to catch anything that falls. The rope or tent pole can help keep the sheet taut.

Even in the middle of Oakland, you should soon have a diverse array of beetles and moths drawn irresistibly to the light's "tractor beam."

The term *arthropods* includes insects (six legs), spiders and scorpions (eight legs), and crabs and barnacles, including one species cluster that we will visit, the fairy or brine shrimp.

Overall, this group is the most numerous, the most species rich, and the most widely distributed—in a word, the most successful—of all animals since the planet began. One can make few statements about nature with certainty, but about the arthropods, we will assert that (1) there are easily ten million species and (2) of this total, many remain undescribed. As a group, insects and arachnids crawl, hop, burrow, wiggle, swim, and fly. The group includes everybody—predators, parasites, herbivores, detritivores, fungivores, and even saproxylics, creatures that make their living eating decaying wood. Insects are colonial or solitary, minute or enormous, dull black or vividly green. As more than one headline has pointed out, "We will miss them when they're gone."

Even if there are only nine million insect species—or six, or who knows, eleven or twelve or thirteen million—half are nocturnal. Unless it is the middle of winter and/or very high in the mountains, insects and spiders and desert shrimp are an expected and abundant part of nature at night. Why come out only then? Some are avoiding desert heat or making good use of humidity or dewfall, but for most species the answer is that they do not want to be gobbled up. Nighttime simply offers more protection than daytime. Over the eons, as more insects switched over to be night-dwellers, plants switched over to producing nectar at night, and predator insects followed the prey base.

Insects at night navigate using starlight, moonlight, and a kind of "bent" wavelength reflected by water, polarized light. The compulsion to stay oriented to moonlight draws them into orbit around the false moons of our porch lights and casino marquees, which is yet another reason why light pollution is not a victimless crime. We will be able to explore that topic better in chapter 10.

In the following portfolios, we will visit arachnids first, then go to creatures usually encountered on the ground or in water, and then end with a sampling of night flyers. The tour will be introductory only, but should show the exciting diversity this part of nature offers.

This three-inch *Prionus* beetle was lured in by a UV black light.

SCORPIONS

Here is a lifestyle and shape that must really work, because scorpions have remained unchanged for 350 million years. During the day, most scorpions wait under brush, bark, or rocks, but after dark they come out to hunt and mate; using a UV flashlight lets you see how many per square meter there truly are. In popular culture they are often the bad guys or equated with malice—in the movie *Lawrence of Arabia*, when Lawrence coolly manipulates Chief Auda in front of his tribe, Auda notes bitterly, "Thy mother mated with a scorpion."

The reality is that they are just regular animals doing regular things, and while the tail does have a stinger with a good zap built into it, it's not lethal to humans (usually). Our largest scorpion, the scarily named giant hairy scorpion, can reach a length of six inches. Most species are only half that size.

Owls, lizards, and snakes eat scorpions. Once the authors were picking apart an owl pellet (the cast-up ball of fur and bones an owl can't digest or poop out) and were puzzled by bits of what looked like pale green plastic. Not plastic: the owl had been eating scorpions, and those were leftover panels of exoskeleton.

It's 9 p.m.—do you know where your children are? (Oh yes, right here.)

This daytime view of a scorpion shows pincers, stinger, and the classic scorpion shape.

All scorpions glow in the dark. This is the same individual from the day shot, but lit with UV light.

Female black widows can be jet black or shades of brown.

BLACK WIDOW SPIDER

The female is the black spider with the red hourglass on its glossy abdomen; males are paler and smaller and, sometimes but not always, the ones that become dessert after mating. (Other spiders do this too, not just the "widows.") The web is robust but not geometric—in one notebook entry, Charles described it as "a scribbled mess." They use these webs to catch wasps, ants, beetles, and other spiders; the range of prey is wide, and if it can get caught in the web, it's likely to get eaten sooner or later. Black widow venom is a serious neurotoxin, and in humans a bite can cause pain, inflammation, and (very rarely) death.

One study wondered whether potential widow-eaters had resistance to black widow venom. Three lizard species that are known to eat black widows—southern alligator lizard, western fence lizard, and side-blotched lizard—were injected with widow venom and tested for their resistance or tolerance.

Only the alligator lizard seemed fine; the other two species did not have natural or acquired protection. The report states, "This is the first study to quantify resistance to any spider venom in natural lizard predators, and the resulting data will help us understand if sympatric lizards have evolved specialized abilities (i.e. toxin resistance) to cope with dangerous prey."

While we stay tuned for the updates, we will mention the little-known fact that the world's largest concentration of black widows is in Charles's garage.

The tarantula hawk lays eggs inside paralyzed tarantulas, yet the adult wasps are vegetarians.

TARANTULAS

Another of our nocturnal friends that haters love to hate, the tarantula is a generally large, generally hairy, generally ground-dwelling spider of open country and worldwide distribution.

Tarantulas in North America are nocturnal hunters. They feed on grasshoppers, beetles, other spiders and arthropods, and sometimes even small lizards. Most tarantula species have venom, though it is fairly dilute. They are not particular about prey and will attempt to overcome anything of the right size that moves in front of them.

Fierce as they look, they suffer from a variety of predators, the most gruesome of which is the tarantula hawk, better called by its

Like Monty Python's Black Knight, this particular tarantula was ready to eat our camera and the car that came with it.

other name, pepsis wasp. The wasp uses olfaction to find a tarantula and stings it underneath, at a weak spot between the joints. This paralyzes it. The wasp then drags it into a nearby burrow before depositing an egg on the abdomen. The wasp seals the spider in the burrow and flies off. The wasp egg hatches into a larva which feeds on the paralyzed spider, eating it from the outside in, heading ever closer to the essential organs, which it eats last.

There may be worse ways to die, but offhand, we can't think of many. Nature—always interesting, but nobody said it was always nice.

THE *OTHER* SPIDERS

All spiders have eight legs, no antennae, and no wings. (Young disperse by "ballooning"—flying on silk parachutes.) Most spiders have venom for subduing their prey and also digesting it, since a spider's mouth has no teeth. Venom can be defensive: "Mess with me and I'll bite you." Spiders drink water (including getting water from moist soil), and most spiders can withstand cold nights by curling up in leaf litter and soil.

Other than these commonalities, spiders exhibit great variety in behavior, habitat, and body-to-leg proportions. Scientists even recently identified a vegetarian spider in Central America.

At night, some, but not all, spiders have eyeshine. We met that term before, in the flashlight discussion. When you scan with a strong flashlight, eyes of night-adapted creatures reflect light. This is true not just for skunks and owls but also for ground-dwellers such as wolf spiders. In fact, in some fields, if you make a slow sweep, it looks as though you're wading into a lake of blue diamonds as a thousand spider eyes catch the light and shine back at you.

This banded garden spider matches exactly what we expect spiders to look like.

Portfolio 2: Other Ground-Dwellers (and One That Swims)

MILLIPEDES

Millipedes are detritus eaters and ground burrowers, and they usually only come out at night, especially after a rainstorm. Each segment of its many-jointed body has two pairs of legs, and the average body length end to end is four or five inches. They grow continuously throughout their life, and each new shedding and reemergence adds another body segment, so any given millipede may have more (or fewer) legs than another one nearby.

The name means "thousand feet," but few millipedes reach that leg count; the previous high count was 750 legs. A newly described millipede species in Australia doubles the average with 1,306 legs.

There are about seven thousand species of millipede in the world, and in a way that cannot be explained, some of them fluoresce in UV light, just the same as scorpions and platypuses. Why? Be sure to let us all know when you sort it out.

WALKING STICKS

Stick bugs or walking sticks (or, more scientifically, phasmids) are insects that look like sticks, but the cool thing is just *how* sticklike they manage to look. Some even rock slightly, just like a twig or leaf rustling in the wind. In case being a mime doesn't work, in a secondary defense, some species can spray a mini-jet of skunk plume from an anterior gland, burning their would-be captors.

Walking sticks are found worldwide, and in the tropics some species get to be two feet long—you can find plenty of online images of these mega-sticks if you're curious (or are morbidly fearful) and want to experience the stuff that dreams (or nightmares) are made of. Not much to be afraid of, really. Stick bugs feed on plants, and some people keep them as pets.

Besides coiling into a defensive ball, a millipede can also emit a foul-smelling chemical.

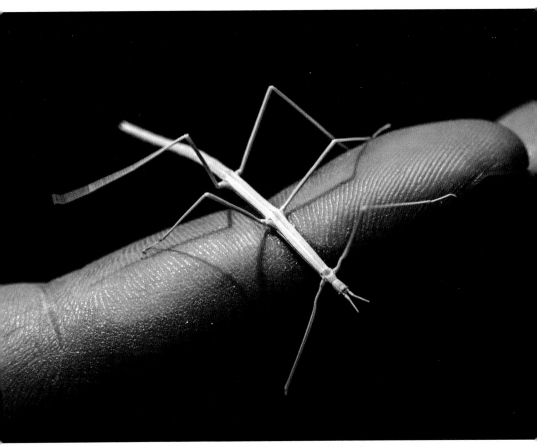

A walking stick found in the California desert explores José's hand.

Pretty bug, but clumsy. It whirrs
loudly and bumbles into things.

GREEN FRUIT BEETLE

Not everything has stingers, venom, or muted colors. This bright-green, inch-long scarab is also called the peach bug, the fig-eating beetle, and other fruit-adjacent names. It is found in the southern tier of the American West. Sweeping up rotting fruit promptly will keep this insect from infesting domestic fruit trees. When it's not looking for backyard fruit, another source of food is mesquite sap.

They may look fierce, but these large, easily observed insects do not bite and don't emit toxins or poisons. To quote one guide to backyard insects, "They are safe to handle and entertaining to watch." We second that, and want to praise the color pattern in particular, with the tan side stripe smartly accenting the green body.

VELVET ANTS

Despite their name, velvet ants are not ants but wasps. There are around seven thousand species worldwide, with dozens in the United States. The group is easily recognized by its flightless, hairy, and often brightly colored females. These nest in the ground, utilizing cavities made by other arthropods. They are easiest to spot during late afternoon or early evening walks, especially in the desert or places with open dirt. (Males are more exclusively nocturnal.)

As wasps, velvet ants have the potential to sting; however, they are not aggressive and are unlikely to react unless handled roughly.

Bright colors warn potential predators about toxicity. Velvet ants can also warn enemies by producing a squeaky noise using organs in their abdomens. A final survival adaptation is their ability to withstand much more physical pressure than other bees or wasps, thanks to their strongly reinforced exoskeleton. Thick armor helps retain moisture and protect against predation. In an ultimate kind of revenge, the body is so tough that it makes it difficult for entomologists to pin dead ones onto collection boards.

The brightly colored velvet ant is actually a wasp.

FAIRY SHRIMP

Summer monsoons in the western United States help form an ephemeral but incredible ecosystem: temporary vernal pools. In addition to the amphibians that we cover later, small arthropods also use this habitat, waiting a full year (or even multiple years) before becoming active with new rain.

Vernal pool inhabitants include fairy shrimp (also called brine shrimp), a group of crustaceans also found in hypersaline bodies of water, such as Mono Lake and Utah's Great Salt Lake. They are not really shrimp but a conglomerate of three hundred species in four different orders. Usually less than an inch long, they have eleven pairs of leaf-shaped legs that they use to swim (belly up) and as paddles for filtering food.

Fairy shrimp eggs are deposited by the millions and can be dormant in the mud for years, surviving drought and hypersalinity, waiting for the rains to form a new pond. Older readers may remember the "sea monkeys" advertised in the back of comic books. Sadly, those were not freeze-dried aliens but simply brine shrimp waiting to be reanimated in your bedroom fishbowl.

Like a spaceship in a starry night, a fairy shrimp swims in a vernal pool. Note the eyes and digestive tract visible inside this transparent animal.

This moth ranges from the Grand Canyon to New Mexico and Texas.

OCULEA SILKMOTH

What a gorgeous insect! The blue and orange in the eyespots on the wings are complementary colors, and the creams and tans match dried oak leaves in the moth's preferred habitat. This is a generously sized moth, and adults can have wingspans up to six inches across. Another name for this species is the western Polyphemus, after the cyclops in Homer's *Odyssey*.

Smell is everything in the moth world, and adults in the mood for love find each other in the dark using species-specific pheromones. To quote T. S. Eliot, "Is it perfume from a dress / That makes me so digress?" The caterpillar of this moth feeds on Emory oak, Mexican blue oak, and Arizona black walnut; adults spend their time looking for mates, but do not feed.

Want to see one yourself? Looking in southwestern forests after a late-day storm clears off is a good way to start. You need two things: a flashlight, and the curiosity to go out after dark and start exploring. Even if you don't see one of these terrific moths, maybe you'll see an owl or a coral snake or a shooting star. It all starts with going out in the first place.

WATER BUGS

Water bugs are ferocious predators and incredible swimmers, yet they also fly, hence inclusion here. Despite looking like beetles, water bugs are more closely related to cicadas, aphids, and leaf-hoppers. The two hundred species represent some of the largest "true bugs." (To specialists, all bugs are not bugs—only *some* bugs are bugs, and these water bugs are among the "true" bugs.) Water bugs are found in freshwater ponds and slow-flowing rivers, where they hunt other invertebrates with their sharp forelimbs and a proboscis that enables them to inject a digestive saliva to liquefy their prey, which they then slurp up. Some of the largest species can even feed on fish, frogs, and snails.

They are easiest to observe at night, using a flashlight to check ponds. They are well camouflaged, but they need to come up to the surface to breathe. For this, they have a breathing tube (a sort of tiny snorkel) that can be retracted into their abdomen. In some species the male carries the fertilized eggs on his back until the moment they hatch. Males with eggs can't fly, so doing this represents a risk and an investment of energy. Yet being protective also means that their genetic flow is more likely to be carried into the future.

Water bugs have received many regional folk names, including "toe-biters" and "alligator ticks." (The only thing more complex and varied than insects is the English language itself.)

Water bugs need to breathe air, so are often found sticking their snorkel-like tubes out of the water, as this one is doing.

Male water bugs carry the eggs on their backs.

Even micromoths can be beautiful when seen up close.

HOLLOW-SPOTTED BLEPHAROMASTIX

Wait, the *what?*

This one makes the book despite being small and utterly obscure, as a stand-in for all the other small, overlooked creatures that populate our nighttime woods and deserts. In fact, it makes the book exactly *because* it is small and obscure. As the ruler indicates in the photo, it is smaller than a US quarter. Lovely colors, though, don't you think? This one came to a UV light and was photographed, and then the light was shut off so it could flit back into the night and continue doing its moth-ish things.

In this paragraph, we would now like to tell you about its life span, list host plants, give conservation and management notes, and maybe share something quirky about mating habits.

We would like to, but we can't.

All-knowing Wikipedia is mute when it comes to this animal, as were eleven websites and three hard-copy reference books. One source did say that larvae once had been found on woodland goosefoot, which is a three-foot-tall native weed. Otherwise, this insect remains terra incognita in the great atlas of life.

The life details of warblers and tanagers were once unknowns too, with observers even wondering whether male and female tanagers were different species. If naturalists can sort out the identification of *Empidonax* flycatchers, why not make some progress on the smaller (but no less valuable) moths of the American West?

Getting More Involved—Ponds after Dark

The fairy shrimp's (page 79) translucent body may make catching it harder for fish and birds. But it also allows us to see their internal structure, including eyes and digestive system. This is easy to do by yourself or as something to share with friends, since fairy shrimp are attracted to light. If you hold a flashlight over a summer pond, fairy shrimp will congregate in the thousands. Scooping them into a glass jar or even just a clean sandwich bag will let you inspect them under a hand lens or by using the macro function on your phone.

Getting More Involved—Winning the Spider Wars

You have probably heard of the "fat bear week" sponsored by Katmai Park in Alaska. As spiders prepare for winter, like bears they become larger and more easily observed. Paralleling the bear event, there is a friendly contest sponsored by the Natural History Museum of London. "We are declaring the next two weeks #FatSpiderFortnight in honor of our eight-legged friends who are out of hiding and looking for love." The museum challenges us to be more alert on walks and around the house so that we can "share pictures of the fattest spiders we can find, using the hashtag #FatSpiderFortnight." At the end of two weeks there is a group vote for the fattest spider, which is to say (just as with bears) the most successful, ecologically.

A black-necked garter snake shows well in the light of a headlamp.

5

LESSONS IN HERPETOLOGY

Keep some room in your heart for the unimaginable.
—**Mary Oliver**

Herps, as they are called by many naturalists, are a large and misunderstood group that includes reptiles and amphibians, which in our region means lizards, snakes, turtles, frogs, toads, and salamanders.

The herp clan is diverse and exciting, yet understudied. For the authors (and we hope for you, too), every snake is a new adventure. Be careful around rattlesnakes, of course—be REALLY careful—but snakes do not deserve to be feared and hated the way they so often are. Luckily, herps do have a fan base. We asked one of the photographers who shot for this book, Tucson-based René Clark, what lures her out night after night to practice her art.

René replied, "I have always been a champion for the underdog and the less-loved creatures of our world. Herps (particularly snakes) hold our imagination hostage and invade our dreams, yet they are also beautiful and beneficial. And let's just face it . . . they are super cool! As a photographer, I am attracted to that lovely combination of power and shyness."

She also admires herps because "they are incredible survivors of climate change, loss of biodiversity and habitat, and human persecution." We agree with her, but we want to use herps as "teachable moments" as well. One of the fun things about nature after dark is how the average hike switches on the less-prioritized senses. Whether one is taking in the smells of night blossoms or hearing (and then seeing) a shrew because of the rustle in leaf litter, being out at night heightens one's nonvisual perceptions. And when one does see an animal in the spotlight, all attention focuses there; even a single tree commands more attention at night than an entire forest typically does during daylight.

Using that idea of focused attention, this chapter will present five ecological ideas that are more easily apprehended by looking for reptiles and amphibians after dark.

Copycats Finish ~~Last~~ First

Batesian mimicry is the term for when one animal that is not poisonous or venomous adopts the warning coloration of another animal that is, in a "false flag" move to convince predators to leave them alone. Three different snakes show this well. With luck, you can see all three of these in one field season, and although you may encounter them during the day, they're more easily seen at night in the summer, especially in the desert.

The Sonoran coral snake (the middle example here) used to be linked to a now-discredited nursery rhyme: "Red on black, friend of Jack; red on yellow, kill a fellow." Coral snakes are venomous and powerfully so, though by temperament and fang shape, they are rarely a threat to humans. (If you are bitten, though, the venom is very potent: seek medical help immediately.)

The top snake of the photo trio is a mountain kingsnake (not venomous), and the bottom one, also not venomous, is called a long-nosed snake. As snakes go, it does have a long-ish nose. These two borrow the coral snake's vivid colors to convince would-be enemies to leave them alone. They are textbook examples of Batesian mimicry.

Which of these three red-and-black snakes is the venomous one?

Bates was a Victorian collector and explorer who worked with Alfred Russel Wallace, the fellow whose codiscovery of the theory of natural selection prompted a reluctant Charles Darwin to publish *The Origin of Species*. After eleven years in the Amazon, Bates had a paperwork job in London for the second half of his life. Wallace always thought that the drudgery of not being able to do daily fieldwork caused Bates's death. Lesson noted. Instead of a hypothetical Gone Fishing sign, what about a sign that says Gone Herping, in Order to Avoid an Early Death? Sounds good to us.

Toxins versus Antitoxins: Who Will Win?

Everybody knows about rattlesnakes, even people who have only seen snakes in movies and cartoons. Some of us maybe even could do a reasonably good sketch of a rattlesnake's gape and its fearsome, venom-injecting fangs. Yet ounce for ounce, the West Coast newts (those adorable "gummy bear" lizards), have just as much killing potential as the longest rattlesnake or brightest poison arrow frog.

Newts such as the two shown on pages 91 and 92 have glands in their skin that secrete the potent neurotoxin tetrodotoxin, which per unit of weight is hundreds of times more toxic than cyanide. (Puffer fish have this same type of toxin.) You should not handle these newts, and if you do, wash your hands immediately afterward. Touching one for a moment won't make you keel over on the spot, but this secretion is not something you want to rub in your eyes or get near your mouth.

Why don't newts succumb to their own poison? The short answer is that newts, poison arrow frogs, and the pitohui (a New Guinea bird) have what researchers call toxin sponges, which are proteins that mop up the fatal toxins before they cause damage. That means they are immune to their own poison. This calls to mind the story of Mithridates, a king who opposed Rome. Fearful

"Look how cute I am. I wouldn't hurt anybody, would I?"

of assassination, he supposedly built up an immunity to poison by ingesting sublethal doses with every meal. (Children, do not try this at home.)

For every defense, there is a new and more determined offense. Garter snakes want to eat newts, and to do so need to be resistant to newts' chemical defenses. The newt in turn needs enough toxin to be inedible but without wasting too much energy creating more chemicals than necessary. There is a cost associated with creating and storing toxin compounds, so you can't be too profligate.

The snake for its part can't risk becoming overly "poison-proof." It's like an army tank. If you put enough armor plating on it so no bomb can penetrate, it becomes too heavy and slow to be useful. With snakes, something similar happens. To quote one research site, "The garter snake's ability to digest poison results in a slower slithering speed, making everyday functions more

The rough-skinned newt is found throughout the Pacific Northwest.

difficult." So for predator and prey, it always is a balancing act—one carried out without either side being conscious that they are part of a millennia-long experiment.

To find a newt, look around streams on rainy nights in spring, turning over rocks and logs. Always put ground cover back where you found it, though; that rock may be creating the right micro-climate above somebody's burrow, even if they're not home now.

When Is a Toad Not a Toad?

For most of us, herp identification skills go as far as "Is it a turtle or is it a frog?" and then stop. A level higher and you might know that a turtle is a reptile, and a frog is an amphibian. The master class knows that toads and frogs are both amphibians, and maybe can tell the two groups apart. After that, for most of us, we're out of choices.

Even if our vocabulary is not animal-rich, we can easily learn to make distinctions. An example of a way to "expand awareness" is to consider the toad look-alikes, the spadefoots.

A spadefoot is neither frog nor toad, but is itself, "spadefoot."

A spadefoot looks like a baby frog or little toadlet, but has its own taxonomic lineage. Unlike true toads (genus *Bufo* et alia), which have knobby warts and horizontal pupils, spadefoot toads have vertical pupils and few or no warts. (And no toad or spadefoot or frog can give you warts if you touch it, but then you knew that.) The typical spadefoot is small—three inches or less—and lives in desert or prairie. It spends most of its life underground, waiting for monsoons to create temporary pools. Interestingly, the cue for adult emergence during these summer thunderstorms is not moisture but the low-frequency sounds and vibration caused by rainfall and thunder, which usually reach their peak in the evening and into the night.

With water comes life, but here it's life highly accelerated: after they emerge, adults have to call, mate, and lay eggs, all in a matter of days, even hours. The eggs hatch into tadpoles same as

Summer monsoons bring good news to the patient spadefoot.

always, but speed-walk their way to adult form. The "spade" of the spadefoot's foot is a special spur that helps it dig. For these animals, digging is essential, since it is soon time to go back underground before the temporary pools dry up completely.

It may seem odd or hard to pay attention to such minor animals as these, but there are several benefits. One of the things that happens to most people when they start birdwatching is that they begin to see (and hear) birds everywhere. Even a walk around the block becomes richer once you learn to hear the chip notes of winter warblers or the *scree scree* of a perched hawk. Those "tells" were there all along, of course. But once you know to *hear* them—to participate in the aural clues fully and mindfully—you realize how much you were previously overlooking.

This applies to the other parts of nature as well, from trees in a park to mushrooms to amphibians. Seeing starts with knowing, and knowing starts with being able to tell a pine from an oak and an oak from an oak titmouse.

Natives, Nonnatives, "Unnatives"

Bullfrogs are native to some parts of North America, are an introduced pest in other parts, and very much are a "does not belong here *at all*" alien species in places such as France, Germany, Italy, Crete, Singapore, Taiwan, and South Korea. How did they get there? Sometimes as escaped pets, but more often it has to do with the fact that the "frog" part of the haute cuisine dish "frog's legs" is almost always the American bullfrog, otherwise known as "it tastes like chicken." By accident or intention, captive frogs intended for the dinner table ended up getting loose and becoming the free-range frogs of ditch and pond, canal and bog. Once loose in a new environment, they are pretty much there to stay.

The soundtrack should be playing the "uh-oh" music from *Jaws*, since nonnative bullfrogs can be really bad news for the lesser and often endemic frogs. Bullfrogs are big and hungry and can breed anywhere. A few escaped bullfrogs quickly become an invading army, and they can eat their way through an entire faunal complex of fish, mammals, and rare frogs.

Yet even if we could wave our magic "bad things be gone" wand, removing the bullfrog from some of these nonnative areas would create new, different problems. The egrets at the Salton Sea do not care about the continent of origin for the bullfrog they just scarfed down. All they know is that they live in a marsh and there never seems to be enough to eat. If bullfrogs help fill in a gap in the menu, then they would say to pass the frog sauce and tuck in.

The American bullfrog has the unfortunate habit of wanting to eat all the frogs smaller than itself, endangered or not.

So then, are nonnative bullfrogs bad for the ecosystems of their new marshlands? Often yes, sometimes no, and too often the answer is, "We're not sure, and we don't know what to do about it anyway."

Good management starts with good data. If you see (or hear) (or catch and eat) a bullfrog, add the record to iNaturalist or the website of your choice. You'll get the most results by checking in the late afternoon and evening, when bullfrogs vocalize most actively. In fact, there is the idea that bullfrogs never sleep, based on how much they call at night and on one often-cited (but flawed) study in 1967. All animals need rest, and whether we call that resting period "sleep" or something else, even bullfrogs need to stop calling and rest sooner or later.

You Don't Know until You Look

We close this chapter with several personal stories. And they all start with this fact: just because we're nature-book authors (and just because José Gabriel does indeed have a doctorate in bat biology), we don't always have good luck every time we go out. Some nights are so slow that we try all our tricks—from Charles putting on his lucky hat to José breaking out his most powerful spotlight—and we still get nothing.

That said, we also have had more than our share of "Well, how about that!" moments. These are the times the puma crosses the road, or you have multiple ringtail sightings in the same night, or you come across a kind of snake nobody ever gets to see in the wild. Such high-five moments count as the best (and sometimes strangest) parts of the nature hike—the moments you can talk about for years afterward. We want you to start having more of these moments too, so we are here to explain a pro tip for how to find the stuff nobody ever sees.

It can be reduced to four words: *Go out and look.*

Sorry, that's all there is to it.

Just start to go out more often, and, it stands to reason, the more often you will come across good, strange, or unexpected things. Here are examples of when that has happened to us.

The first story is of a time when the authors were birding in the Texas Hill Country. Both of us like this kind of habitat, but we do not know it well. There are the drier, juniper-covered hillsides, and then the sycamores and maple trees of the lusher, more botanically dense streams and rivers. Clear, shallow rivers flow across white limestone shelves, and we guessed that these streams would be good for herping, but had been haphazard in our planning. What would we find? Time to put on hip waders and headlamps and find out.

Small problem. We didn't have any hip waders. That was an oopsie in packing.

Forget your hip waders? Charles says, "Go out anyway."

No matter: it was a warm night, and modern hiking clothes dry quickly. Time to follow the implied second rule: *Go out anyway.* So what if you get a bit wet and muddy? Just try not to track it on the carpet when you get back to the motel.

We heard screech owls and great horned owls, and our bat detector had plenty of hits, so we felt like things were hopping. The air was filled with the sound of crickets and chorus frogs, and, distantly, almost as if on cue, Bruce Springsteen's "Thunder Road" echoed from a passing car. Flickers of fireflies danced into view and evaporated just as quickly. A light breeze was keeping the mosquitoes from settling—good thing, since in another *oh shoot dang* moment, I had left the mozzie spray in the room. Somewhere in a backyard, a barbecue was getting fired up—we had not had dinner, and the smell of wood smoke reminded us of that keenly.

Eyeshine—a raccoon was watching us from a hole in a bald-cypress. Following a second raccoon brought us to what can be called "The Great Battle of Snake versus Frog." This second raccoon had dashed off, but where it had disappeared, something was thrashing in the shallow water. Looking closer, we saw that it was a snake—no, it was a snake trying to eat a frog.

We watched in a mix of fascination and horror as a water snake tried to eat a Rio Grande leopard frog, except that the snake had gripped the frog hind legs first, which meant that the frog was turned around the wrong way and so could not be easily swallowed. The frog's head was almost as big as the snake's, but the snake was determined to find a way to make it fit. Normally we are pro-snake on our nighttime rambles, but this case was more macabre than usual, since the frog in question was (1) endangered and (2) conscious the entire time. Did we want the frog to wiggle free? (Maybe.) Should we try to intervene? (Probably not.) Right or wrong, in the end the snake won.

As we waded along the shore and took detours into the thickets, we ended up seeing another water snake, and another, and a toad, and one more water snake, and two white-tailed deer. One red fox. A herd of nonnative but smartly attractive fallow deer. But the real surprise is documented by the photo on the next page, after José spotted a Texas blind snake.

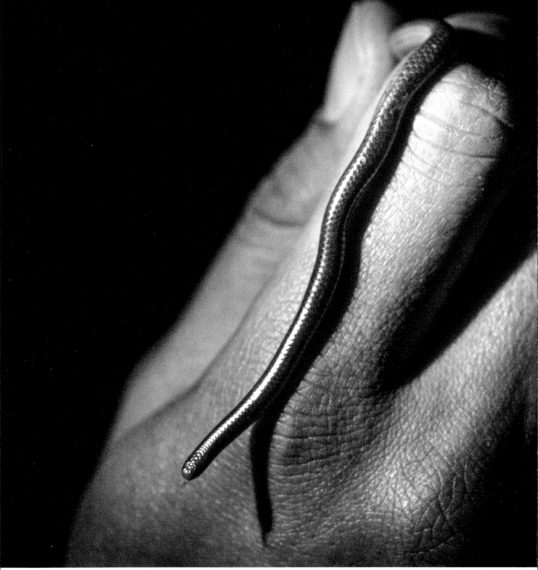

Worm or snake, both or neither? (See text for answer.)

As snakes go, this one hardly even seemed like a reptile, since it had the glossy texture and pink color of a big, juicy worm. When we first saw it, the surprise created one of my favorite moments in nature study: an instantaneous collision of "Wow, how cool," followed by "What the heck *is* it?"

After a bit of discussion, we figured it out. With this species, the flicking tongue is almost too small to see, and the vestigial eyes are covered by translucent scales. Blind snakes rarely come to the surface and instead live what field guides call a fossorial lifestyle, meaning they spend all their time burrowing under the surface. This species was new to us both, and props to José Gabriel, whose fast hands nabbed it before it could slip away.

We took our pictures, went *oohh* and *aahh*, and released it in the leaf litter. What a great find!

The next example occurred when José Gabriel was driving at night with Erin Westeen, a herpetologist studying at UC Berkeley. They were in the Mojave National Preserve, a few miles east of Baker. They took the sidewinder photograph we see on pages 102–3. It was up in a bush, but should not have been . . . that is not the usual sidewinder habitat.

Sidewinders are those pale rattlesnakes whose wriggling body leaves hook-marked tracks on the face of sand dunes, as if somebody has been practicing cursive J's over and over. This "side-winding" motion helps the snake minimize contact with hot surfaces in summer, cold surfaces in winter, and loose, hard-to-grip sand slopes year-round.

Young sidewinders mostly eat lizards (which they sometimes lure in with a waggle of their tail); larger sidewinders eat lizards, rodents, birds, nestlings, and snakes. Females give birth in a rodent burrow (after eating the occupants first), and during the heat of the day, summer sidewinders retreat to burrows or else bury themselves in the sand under a dense bush. None of that behavior includes much arboreal activity. And it was a spring night, a time when one might expect snakes to be staying on the warm asphalt, not draping themselves over the crown of a prickly plant whose other common name is burroweed.

So given all that, what was this snake doing in a bursage shrub? Maybe warming up (or cooling down), maybe hoping for a sleeping bird, or maybe it didn't know—just doing what José and Erin were doing, which was trying to see what possibilities the night had to offer.

Sidewinders are dune-adapted rattlesnakes, though this one inexplicably is cruising through white bursage.

Another rule for our growing list: *When in doubt, always take a picture.* Follow that photo with a few quick notes, even if it's just as a phone memo to yourself. You should write down the date, time, air temperature, where you are, and what the beastie in question had been doing (which in this case was baffling the science crew).

What that means in this case is that the two biologists did what anybody should do, which was to get close (but not *too* close) and document behavior with a good flash and a telephoto lens. Don't have those? Then smartphone it is, in which case you can upload your iNaturalist report at the same time. And after we checked several hundred posts, it seems that out of all the recent sidewinder photographs, only one other photo shows the snake in a bush (and, in fact, in this same species of bush, white bursage).

The aggregate power of all us working together via data sharing may lead to exciting discoveries in the years ahead.

Is it just us, or does this toad look like Winston Churchill?

A great horned owl silhouetted in a saguaro waits to start his day.

6

OWLS, NIGHTHAWKS, AND NIGHTJARS

Sometimes an owl is just an owl.
—**Mark Frost,** ***The Secret History of Twin Peaks***

From Pallas Athena to Harry Potter, there are more owls in literature than sparrows, eagles, and mockingbirds combined. Is it because they look like us? If so, it all starts with the head. Just as ours do, an owl's eyes face forward, locked into a face-like skull; the sharp beak is small and often lost in feathers, while the round facial disc can look serene, angry, wise, or blank, depending on the species and on the expectations of the observer. *Owls in Hell*— that could be the title of a book about the art of Hieronymus Bosch, while in the comic poetry of Edward Lear, the owl and the pussycat go to sea in a pea-green boat (and then get married).

If you like owls and you live in (or plan to visit) North America, you and your bird list are in luck. Ornithologists list a total of thirty-three nightbirds in North America, including twenty-three species of owls. These range from the sparrow-sized elf owl, the smallest raptor in the world, on up to the great gray owl, a bird so powerful it can punch through two feet of snow in order to reach a burrowing vole.

After owls, the tally next includes three kinds of night-hawk: common, lesser, and, in the Florida Keys, the Antillean nighthawk, a bird whose call is *pity-pit-pit*. Birders who go there and can't find one cry *pity* a lot too.

And last, when it comes to the nightjars, we have seven in North America, counting East Coast species and Alaskan strays. What's a nightjar? Ah yes, good question, and our cue to get into examples and specifics. Let's take a deeper look at the three nightbird groups now.

Owls

The generic owl is tree-bark brown; it has asymmetrical ears (for better sound triangulation) and ultrasoft (and hence silent-in-flight) body feathers. The round facial disc is another way to gather sound, like a radar dish. Owl eyes are fixed in place and provide excellent depth perception. To look behind itself, an owl can swivel its head 270 degrees. And what eyes! An owl can see in the dark as well as the average person can see at high noon.

The typical owl eats rats, voles, and mice, though snakes and fish and hares and insects make it onto the menu, depending on the season and which species is involved.

Owl pellets are bundles of hair and fur that the roosting owl coughs up during the day, since there are always parts of every dinner that are too sharp or too coarse for them to poo out the regular way. These don't smell bad—they are not icky, like dog mess—and if you break them open, you can discover what the owl has been eating. You also can use them to find the owl itself. Most owls roost in trees during the day, and to find a daytime owl—for example, in your local park—look for the pellets on the ground under a big tree. If the grass is watered often, the pellets break down quickly, but you usually still can see the white bones and a small slurry of gray fur—an overwatered owl pellet looks like wet papier-mâché.

Once you find pellets, there are often some splashes of white-wash on intervening branches that can be further corroboration.

Western screech owls are robin sized and typically live in oak woodlands. Their tooting call sounds like a bouncing Ping-Pong ball.

All owls cough up pellets of hair and bone. You can break them open to see what the owls have been eating.

Then it's just a matter of standing still and looking. Odds are, the owl is up there somewhere, and may be looking right back down at you at the same time. Remember, they're camouflaged to blend in, so it can be hard to spot a roosting owl that is tucked up high in complicated branches. Or it may be that no matter how hard you look, it won't help, since owls can use multiple roost trees.

Even so, now you know where to look next time, and don't forget to put some pellets in a bag to dissect at home.

Here is an overview of owl species of the American West, sorted from large to small.

GREAT HORNED OWL

You've almost certainly heard this species—*hoo HOO*—and probably have seen it too: a large owl with ear tufts that roosts in trees by day, but at dusk often perches in the open (even on streetlights and rooftops) before going out to hunt.

Great horned owls occur everywhere, from desert ledges to swampy meadows to city parks. They primarily eat mammals—rabbits, skunks, mice, wood rats, pet cats—but are large of appetite and generous of mood, so will also have a go at snakes, coots, doves, fish, and bats. As noted in an earlier chapter, they even eat scorpions.

Pairs stay together year-round, and unless one dies, they will remain together through successive seasons. (If a mate dies, the survivor stays on territory and waits for a replacement to hoot its way into her or his heart.) They nest early in spring and before trees leaf out, so late winter or early spring can be good times to look for this species, since they vocalize at dusk and often can be easily seen. They will respond to a playback of their own calls, but please be brief and judicious, or better yet, don't do it at all.

As blue dusk deepens, a great horned owl gets ready to hunt.

BARN OWL

This is a cinnamon-backed, white-bellied bird, and in a car's high beams, it looks whiter still. The face is heart shaped rather than disc round, which is one way to ID them, and barn owls (like the one shown here) do indeed like to roost in old barns.

They hunt in open areas, including agricultural fields, meadows and heaths, marshes, and desert washes. They can turn up in surprising places. In Berkeley, barns are scarce, yet barn owls thrive, mostly by roosting in Canary Island palms—some of which are 120 years old and so are both tall and frond dense. Barn owls also can be seen in downtown Los Angeles (and get misreported at times as lost snowy owls).

Barn owls have a dish-shaped face that helps focus sound.

Barn owl says, "Silly humans, go back to bed—it's not dark yet."

An elongated posture and a surprised look are typical of long-eared owls.

LONG-EARED OWL

This one looks like a great horned owl but is smaller, slimmer, and more stretched out. Some field guides call them "lanky." Ear tufts are taller than a great horned owl's on average, and the face is more orange. In winter they aggregate in loose roosting flocks and don't mind fairly low (but dense) hedgerows of salt cedar; in summer they can roost in loose associations as well, though in summer, finding a pair defending a solitary nest is just as common. They nest in tree crooks, dense brambles of mistletoe, on cliff ledges, or in cavities in dead trees.

Long-eared owls eat smaller-sized prey than great horned owls, with an emphasis on voles, kangaroo rats, pocket gophers, and young rabbits. It has such acute hearing that it can capture prey in complete darkness.

Coming to a marsh near you: the attractive but crepuscular short-eared owl.

SHORT-EARED OWL

Dawn and dusk, floating over a meadow or marsh—that is the time and place to watch for short-eared owls. They have a round face and a coursing flight as they zigzag silently over open landscape, only to drop with utter precision on a vole or muskrat. They are yellower and streakier than a barn owl, and broader winged in relation to its body size than another marsh-hunting raptor, the northern harrier or marsh hawk. (Harriers have a facial disc too, but always have a longer body with a pale rump. Female harriers are owl brown, and males are pearly gray; both sexes always have a white rump flash.)

This owl's face is very distinctive, with kohl-rimmed eyes and an outline of white setting off the full facial disc. A subspecies of short-eared owl lives only in Hawaii, where the indigenous name is *pueo.*

The boreal owl is probably not rare—it is just rarely seen by people.

BOREAL OWL

Small and strictly nocturnal, this owl remains a blank spot on many birders' lists. The "boreal" name fits well; one axis of the range map starts in New Mexico and follows the Rockies northwest to Alaska, and the other arm follows the forests of Canada east to the Maritimes. It also occurs in Europe where it is known as Tengmalm's owl, named for a Swedish biologist who died of dysentery.

The female can be twice as heavy as the male. The usual explanation for this sexual dimorphism is that two sizes make parents better hunters, since they have different capabilities. The larger females also may be able to better defend the nest, including against any males who suddenly become interested in bite-sized owlet snacks. Last, females need to be able to lay and incubate a clutch of eggs, so size helps there too.

This saw-whet owl has just caught a vole in a woodpile (and isn't about to give it up to the photographer).

SAW-WHET OWL

Tuu, tuu, tuu—the northern saw-whet owl's call sounds like somebody sharpening a saw with a whetstone, or at least it did to naturalists in the nineteenth century.

Mary Freeman is the queen of owl surveys in the Los Angeles mountains. Saw-whets are her particular favorite. She says, "Once in the hand, the beauty of this small owl is utterly captivating." She especially likes the name in Spanish: *la chusita cabezon*, the "big-headed small owl."

Saw-whets breed in all the mountains of the American West. In winter, some stay put and some wander, usually no farther than the middle states, but sometimes all the way to the Gulf Coast and northern Florida.

Mary Freeman: "This endearing bird steals another bit of my heart each time I see it."

The whiskered screech owl eats mice, moths, and beetles. The stiff feathers around the beak are called rictal bristles and help the bird sense insects in the dark.

SCREECH OWLS

Another TWN—"totally wrong name," as humans mislabel nature yet again. Not one of the screech owl species screeches; typical vocalizations are whinnies and trills, and the western screech owl's call sounds like a dropped Ping-Pong ball, starting slowly at first and then bouncing faster and faster. (According to one guidebook, the whinny of an eastern screech owl resembles "a horse on helium.")

Screech owls have small ear tufts and middleweight status; they're eight inches long, so are not dinky and yet not super-size-me either. The whiskered screech owl is an Arizona specialty, while the western screech owl is the expected small owl in riparian corridors and oak woodlands. A habitat "omnivore," it ranges from saguaro to montane pines.

A western screech owl waits for the authors to turn off their flashlights so it can continue hunting in peace.

Most birders see their first elf owl in Arizona's Madera Canyon, where this photo documents a successful hunt.

ELF OWL

This sparrow-sized, one-ounce owl is the Thumbelina of the borderlands. It nests in saguaro holes, in oaks and sycamores along desert streams, and in phone poles, fence posts, nest boxes, and yucca stalks. As much as we try to avoid terms like "cute" in this book, in the spring, males don't hoot or growl—they vocalize with high-pitched, puppy-like yips.

Food can be captured midair or on the ground, and primarily consists of moths, crickets, scorpions, centipedes, and beetles, with the sharp barbs and other pointy bits plucked off before noshing. Elf owls are small enough and nimble enough

Typical flight view of a lesser nighthawk, showing the mottled plumage and white wing flashes.

to hang off of flowers to look for insects, and can run for short distances on the ground. Young rodents and small reptiles such as blind snakes (page 100) get taken as well. They will drink water when they can, but can do without if they have to (and seemingly thrive).

Bird banders take note: elf owls do not like being handled and may feign death until released.

Nighthawks

As the poet Yusef Komunyakaa says, nighthawks "scissor edges of twilight, cutting / black shapes into sky." These are cigar-bodied, arc-winged aerial hunters that come out at dusk to start chasing any insect that flies. They loop and bank, rising up high and diving down low to swing around again—not like the quirk and jink of bats, but more like the sprints and dips of swifts and swallows.

Their long wings have white flashes that can be seen when they swing close to a stadium's lights (or that can be caught in your flashlight's beam).

Of the two species found here, both are actually robin sized, though in the air they look as big as kestrels, since there is nothing to compare them against and the wing flashes grab one's attention. The common nighthawk goes *peent, peent* and mostly is seen around forests and meadows; the lesser nighthawk has slightly different wing crescents and is more open country and desert in emphasis, including the urban desert of the Las Vegas Strip. These are summer visitors only; both species migrate to South America during the northern winter, and strays have turned up as far away as Great Britain. Folk names for common

There are two birds here: mother and chick. Because they have such cryptic plumage, nighthawks on the ground are almost invisible.

nighthawk include bull-bat, pisk, and pork-and-beans, which is to say, god bless rustics and moonshiners, and won't y'all come back and rename all the other birds for us, too?

Both nighthawk species nest on the ground, barely bothering to make a little unadorned scrape. When it comes to modest, easily overlooked nests, nighthawks know that "less is more."

Nightjars

Here is a rhetorical question from the novelist Jonathan Franzen, who ranks nightjars high among his favorite bird groups. "What's not to like about birds that are all but impossible to find by daylight, give spooky and/or beautiful calls at dusk, and operate so gorgeously in the dark?" And the answer is that there is nothing not to like and everything to love.

How spooky is the call? Night hiker John Lewis-Stempel, writing about the European nightjar, reports that its "territorial calling travels half a mile or more, and seems to come from every direction at once—the original surround sound."

Worldwide there are one hundred nightjar species, and most are robin sized, though in headlights they can look larger. All nightjars are covered in a swirly mix of tans and grays, and in the words of one birdwatcher, nightjars "look like a moth that made a wish to become a bird."

Most nightjars nest on the ground, usually just in a small, unlined scrape, and all year long they spend the daytime hours resting, protected by their camouflaged plumage. At dusk their workday begins, and for the rest of the night, nightjars use their superb vision and huge mouths to scoop up flying insects such as grasshoppers, beetles, and moths. As with some of the owl species too, rictal bristles around the base of the bill work like a cat's whiskers to detect prey and protect the eyes.

The group name comes because their ventriloquial calls supposedly "jar" the night. When being formal, some birders

Poorwills hunt from open areas, such as little-used dirt roads.

and most ornithologists use the term *caprimulgids*. More fun is the now-dated term *goatsuckers*, since supposedly with their wide beaks they sucked milk from goat udders. Another grand not-trueness is the medieval idea that nightjars hibernated in the bottoms of ponds, which was a way of explaining where European birds went in winter. They actually went to Central Africa and got there the regular way, by flying across the Sahara, no goat udders or pond mud involved at all.

We are blessed with three nightjar species in the American West: the poorwill, the Mexican whip-poor-will, and an Arizona specialty, the buff-collared nightjar. You can tell them apart by voice, and listening online or in the field, you can almost hear the mournful imperative, *whip poor WILL*. Habitat is a guide to identification as well. Poorwills are more expected in deserts and rocky canyons, and whip-poor-wills in forests.

One surprise occurred in 1944, when biologist Edmund Jaeger discovered that poorwills could go into winter torpor—in essence, a modified kind of hibernation. (We now know that hummingbirds do this on cold nights, as do lesser nighthawks.) A torpid poorwill can reduce its oxygen consumption by 90 percent, and some poorwills spend most of the winter in a state of partial or full dormancy.

You usually see nightjars in car headlights while you drive summer back roads at night. Nightjars don't patrol meadows and forest edges the way owls do. Instead, they will wait in an open area—such as a dirt road or forest clearing—and then sally out from there. Sometimes they use a fence post or tree stump as a perch, but they do not soar and glide the way a nighthawk does—they are more like a phoebe or a flycatcher than a swift or a swallow.

Cultural references to whip-poor-wills or their calls occur in everything from the poetry of Emily Dickinson to the stories of William Faulkner to the ballads of Hank Williams.

Are you so lonesome you could cry? This is the group of birds made just for you.

Getting More Involved—Elf Owl Surveys

Saguaro National Park has saguaros and it has elf owls, but how many owls and how best to manage them—that is a topic the rangers need help with. There is too much habitat for them to survey on their own.

Community volunteers help out by walking transects in teams and listening for (and often seeing) elf owls, as well as another small owl, the western screech. They also can expect to run across coyotes, great horned owls, and scorpions. As the call for volunteers explains, "You must have reasonably good hearing and be comfortable walking a trail at night while using a headlamp or flashlight. These two surveys are scheduled near the full moon to try and have as much light as possible but it will still be quite dark out there!" This is a good way to help science and to walk at night with experienced, like-minded companions. The collective total often surpasses two hundred elf owls tallied in one season.

Getting More Involved—Attracting Barn Owls (Even If You Don't Have a Barn)

If you want to attract a barn owl to your yard or park, they do take up residence in human-made nest boxes. Online there are dozens of kits and plans, as well as ads for the ready-made box itself. The nest box can be mounted on a tree, building, or tall pole. There are lots of reasons to want owls around, the most obvious of which is that they mean you won't need poison to deal with rats. But we like them for another reason: barn owls make the most deliciously eerie calls of any night animal in this book. One reference website says the barn owl's mating call is "a drawn-out gargling scream . . . often given many times in sequence." According to experts, this species also snores, hisses, squeals, and screeches. Do your neighbors ever annoy you? Now you know how to get even.

This fierce ball of lint is on its way to becoming an adult great horned owl.

Ready to start? A hummingbird lifts off into the night.

7

MIGRATION
THE INVISIBLE RIVER

All good trips are, like love, about being carried out of
yourself and deposited in the midst of terror and wonder.
—**Pico Iyer**

Bats do it, dragonflies do it, humpback whales do it, and of
course many birds do it, although some birds do it by walking,
not flying, in the case of altitudinal migrants such as mountain
quail. Worldwide, billions of birds move around the planet chasing (or avoiding) rainfall or just following the sunlight to better
and more abundant seasons. And they do much of this long-haul
travel at night, or else by flying day *and* night, no rest.

In a calendar year, a sooty shearwater covers forty thousand
miles in a figure-eight migration route. This is an ashy-brown
seabird the size and shape of a small, acrobatic seagull. It feeds on
the wing—either riding the wind to "shear" the face of the waves
or diving underwater to catch fish and squid. This species nests
in burrows in New Zealand and Tierra del Fuego, coming ashore
after dark. After the nesting season, New Zealand's shearwaters
diagonal across the Pacific, following the winds to richer feeder
grounds up north during the austral winter.

Another bird flies nonstop the other way, breeding in Alaska
and ending up in New Zealand, where our winter is the austral
summer. Bar-tailed godwits, large shorebirds with rapier-slim

These sandhill cranes are leaving Alaska to head to the Lower 48.
Some will migrate as far as the Texas coast.

Pacific golden plovers winter in Hawaii, then like the godwits, migrate nonstop across the ocean to breeding territories in Alaska.

beaks, can't glide like shearwaters, nor can they bob in the water like gulls. To reach Australia and New Zealand, bar-tailed godwits have to fly . . . and fly and fly and fly, flapping their wings for 240 hours without rest.

We know about these journeys thanks to solar-powered location trackers, which provide data in real time. The bar-tailed godwits' flight paths include one route that requires the longest nonstop migration of any known bird.

Even birds as small as hummingbirds (total weight, less than a penny) migrate long distances. Heading to wintering grounds in Mexico and Central America, the ruby-throated hummingbird crosses the Gulf of Mexico in a nonstop five-hundred-mile flight. Migration fills the night with invisible, crisscrossing rivers of life—even if we never directly witness most of the actual movement.

Nashville Warblers (Are Not from Nashville)

While high-tech trackers let us know the movement of shore-birds, most of what we know about bird movement comes from bird banding efforts, an activity that is called "ringing" in Europe. This three-photo sequence shows how the process usually works.

We are at Bear Divide, a low pass in the mountains near Los Angeles. Most days in spring, thousands of birds cross over this narrow gap in the mountains. Over the counting season of spring 2022, thirty thousand birds were censused passing through Bear Divide, representing 140 species. While most were counted on the wing, some weekends fine mesh nets were set up as well. Birds are not used to looking for these and fly into the "mist" nets, get tangled up, and have to await extraction by banders. You need training and a permit in order to handle migratory birds this way; bats are studied like this too.

Image 1 on page 134 shows a Nashville warbler caught in the banders' net. Ignore the "Nashville" part—this species winters in Mexico, migrates across much of the Lower 48, and breeds in the Sierras, the Cascades, and parts of eastern Canada. Each spring it has to move north, which is how it ended up in a net at Bear Divide. After being weighed and measured (image 2), the bird received a fitted and numbered band, which was installed with a special pair of crimping pliers. Anywhere in the world, if the bird shows up alive or dead, the finder can copy the band number and send it to Washington, D.C. This will allow researchers (and the finder) to learn where the bird was banded originally and how many years have elapsed.

In image 3, the warbler is ready to be released. Time from net capture to release varies (and is longer if a lot of birds go into the nets at once), but might only be a few moments total. Workers try to be swift yet gentle, and birds seem to suffer no harm from their detour through the banding process. When released, most fly to the nearest bush, maybe preen for a moment, and then carry on with their day.

Recovered bands help determine life spans in the wild—from four or five years for most songbirds to thirty-three years for one particularly robust Canada goose. Wisdom, a female Laysan albatross, was first banded in 1956 on Midway Atoll, near Hawaii. She is in her seventies now, and as of when we went to press, Wisdom was still alive and raising chicks.

A migrating warbler is caught in a bander's mist net.

A numbered band is crimped around the bird's leg.

This Nashville warbler, freshly banded, is ready for release.

How Do Birds Get Around in the Dark?

We know how we get to a new place, and the usual way is to let Siri take us there. But how do birds do it? Answer: by using the planet's magnetic field ("magnetoreception"), the position of the sun, internal star maps checked against the night sky, memory, smell, and "factor x," which is to say, parts of migration remain a mystery. Birds are smart, and birds can learn, remember, and make conscious choices. They get around better the more often they have done it before, and even an off-route bird (one that ends up in the wrong place) may return the next year and the one after that, if the conditions are favorable. Some wintering birds even come back to the same tree.

One way that birds navigate is by "seeing" the magnetic field of the Earth, using receptors in the eye. For humans driving at night, we know to stay in our freeway lane based on the visual clue of the painted lines and the tactile clue of the ceramic markers ("Botts' dots"). Stray out of the approved path, and *bumpa bumpa*, you feel (and hear) your tires running over the lane markers, and you know to pull back onto the correct path.

Migratory birds know which lane they are in because they "see" the magnetic lines that wrap around the Earth. Magnetic north is a distinct place, and one can make a longitude and latitude grid using it as an anchor point. (For those of us who have not used an analogue compass, it points not to true north but to magnetic north, and old-school topographic maps had a little diagram at the bottom so you could correct the declination.) Even a young bird can follow this magnetic orientation, so even if it won't know exactly how far to go or what it is looking for at the end of the route, it will still know that south is "over yonder."

Earlier (page 31) we looked at how moonlight and night animals interact. The Moon influences migration as well. According to a study in Sweden, European nightjars hunt more actively on moonlit nights, but also are more likely to begin migrating then too. That is partly because the increased food intake prepares

As the Earth rotates, the stars pivot in a circle centered on the North Star. In this time-lapse image, the straight lines are satellites.

them for the journey, but it also implies that they can more expertly navigate using moonlight.

The "why" of nocturnal migration is easier to explain than the "how." By migrating at night, birds avoid diurnal predators (peregrine falcons, Cooper's hawks), extreme heat when crossing deserts, and (to a lesser extent) the most turbulent winds. They also can feed during the day and use the stars at night for backup navigation.

It may seem amazing to us now that a sparrow can migrate thousands of miles and do it unerringly, and do it all in the dark. Yet one thing to remember is that before smartphones, humans were fairly good at getting around as well, if we think about long-distance Polynesian ocean voyages or even the team of Lewis and Clark, who walked from St. Louis to the Pacific Ocean and back without roads or maps. They may not have known the way, but their Native American guides did. Henry David Thoreau was an abolitionist, and as part of the Underground Railroad, he helped enslaved people escape to Canada. After dark he would hitch up a wagon and take them to train stations, buy them their tickets, and make sure they got away safely. Traveling in the dark was second nature to him, and not just to him but to almost all other rural people before streetlights and smartphones.

These days, many people are unsure which way north is in relation to where they are standing, and some folks can't even find their parked car without help. Is the Moon waxing or waning? Will there be an eclipse this year? Maybe we should all be more like birds: every so often we should step into a clear area, look around, and orient ourselves to the Sun, the Moon, and the stars above.

Community Science and Migration

Two interesting projects allow nonscientists to contribute to migration studies.

The first option is to record flight calls at night. As flocks migrate, small birds use high-pitched "chip" notes to keep track of one another.

"You still over there, Joe?"

"Cheep, cheep, yes I am. Watch out for that owl!"

Migrant birds may also give snippets of territorial songs. Researchers call this medley of collective sounds "nocturnal flight calls" (NFCs). This is not new, of course. Indigenous Americans have been noting the passage of migrant birds for thousands of years; in the Anglo-European tradition, in North America formal study started in 1899, when Orin Libby counted thirty-six hundred calls from night-migrating birds in five hours of listening.

Received tradition is that listening for NFCs is more productive in the eastern United States, due to lower cloud ceilings and more concentrated woodland migrants. Yet there is a growing set of volunteers trying it in the western US as well. The *Journal of Arizona Field Ornithologists* reports that for one volunteer, out of "72 nights recorded, [his] preliminary analysis documented a total of 20,994 passerine NFCs."

To record the calls, put an iPhone in a bucket on your balcony and let it run all night, recording whatever it hears. (The bucket amplifies and focuses sound.) To analyze findings later, there are various software bundles, which include ways to identify hundreds of bird species. Fancier options include using dedicated microphones and high-capacity digital recorders.

Not everything calls or sings in flight; vireos and flycatchers are typically more silent. But one advantage of keeping an "ear" open for NFCs is that some birds, such as grasshopper sparrows, are undercounted simply because they're hard to find. Yet NFC searches revealed more of them passing overhead than visual searches have documented. Another advantage is that documenting nocturnal migration can help conservation. Bright buildings harm migrants (causing them to become disoriented and fly into towers, bridges, and skyscrapers), and the data about what birds fly when may help persuade urban planners not to overlight tall structures.

To learn more, there is an NFC Facebook group and of course the inevitable YouTube videos, as well as sound libraries to help with identification. Recording at night means you will pick up other things too—frogs, dogs, and helicopters, to name three common layers of static. There are ways to filter out those extraneous sounds, and hence—like the nuggets of gold left in the bottom of the miner's pan—end up with just the good stuff. If your luck is like that of some of the other volunteers we know, in a few nights of audio surveying you can expect to end up with recordings of Swainson's thrushes, barn owls, lazuli buntings, and savannah sparrows.

Another way to watch migration in real time is to look at the face of the full Moon with a birding scope. "Moonwatching" may

Flying in a V reduces drag, as these migrating whimbrels demonstrate.

seem like a way to prank newbies (or else the title for a series of Japanese woodblock prints), but it is indeed a real thing. Kimball Garrett of the Natural History Museum of Los Angeles County says this: "Try scoping the face of the moon for a couple of ten-minute periods and recording the number of birds you see passing across the moon's disk. (Sunglasses or some kind of filter on your scope would be helpful.) Recording the direction of movement—e.g., with the moon's face as an analog clock, writing down '7:00 to 1:00' or '5:00 to 12:00'—can help pin down the orientation of the migrants."

Some observers have tried making videos to be sure they're not missing anything, since they can play footage back in slow-mo later. Other moonwatchers know to check the phase of the Moon against migration prediction resources, such as the website BirdCast.

If you try this yourself, at the very least you will have had a chance to study the Moon for half an hour, which we think is always a good thing.

Birds Migrate at Night—or Do They?

Richard Crossley, a British birder and author of the Crossley ID Guides, has been studying migration in what he calls the "Golden Triangle," where Kern County meets Los Angeles County along Interstate 5. When it comes to migration, he is a bit contrarian and rejects a simplistic "migrate at night, rest during the day" narrative.

In birding chat rooms, he has developed a set of alternatives, starting with this claim: "I believe it is best not to think of migrants as 'diurnal' and 'nocturnal.' Birds are migrants simply trying to move long distances from A to B the best way they can."

To Crossley, nocturnal migration is more complex. He says, "Birds adapt to the weather and food that is available. Their routes vary, depending on the circumstances. Trans-Gulf migrants, usually arriving over land midday, nearly always keep flying when the weather is suitable. This is one of almost limitless examples in the Northern Hemisphere that suggest the term 'nocturnal migrants' is inappropriate." He says this because "most birds appear to fly through the first part of the night and then rest for a few hours. They take off at first light to start migrating again, presumably putting down in the afternoon to rest and feed before taking off again at dark."

In his data, cloudy days showed less migration. He thinks birds are strongly influenced by the sun, because "(a) the sun's heat helps with uplift, thus conserving energy; (b) the position of the sun helps birds navigate; and (c) the sun attracts insects/ food."

Interstate 5 passes next to the Los Angeles River near Dodger Stadium, yet despite traffic, community science efforts here have recorded buntings, warblers, and thrushes migrating overhead.

Wind direction matters too. Crossley suggests that "migrating birds fly into the wind. This helps them feed, controlling their speed and helping with uplift. They 'hopscotch'—feed for up to a minute and then fly several hundred yards to stop and feed again. This seemingly arbitrary behavior is remarkably consistent. Some species tend to move a bit quicker between stops than others, [which is] a great project to investigate [someday]." In other words, here again is that same phrase we have heard so often before: "more study needed."

Our photograph on page 142 of a western tanager seems to tie into Crossley's ideas about stop-and-start migration, and how birds don't just follow a "fly at night, rest by day" formula. One spring Charles and José were camping in Jawbone Canyon, at the western edge of the Mojave Desert. Expected species in this habitat are LeConte's thrashers and black-throated sparrows (and antelope ground squirrels and yellow-backed spiny lizards). This site is unambiguously desert. Western tanagers, by contrast, winter in the tropics and nest in the pine forests of the Sierra. They are not desert birds, not if they can help it.

Dawn came, and a western tanager flew into camp. One assumes this particular bird was not where it expected to be. The bird's first thought probably was, "Wait—where are all the green trees?" No matter: it fed on small moths in the rabbitbrush and sage, and after half an hour, it lifted off and carried on north out of sight. As Crossley says, it was migrating at night, but also migrating *not* at night.

Good luck, little fellow—and may the Force (and good tailwinds) be with you.

A migrating western tanager has just caught a moth.

Jawbone Canyon in the Mojave Desert—a good place for camping, for astrophotography, for seeing kangaroo rats, and, in spring, for seeing migration in action.

A canyon bat swoops low over a pond for a drink.

8

THE TRUTH ABOUT BATS

Win friends, not battles. —**bat expert Merlin Tuttle explaining his approach to conservation**

You won't see many exclamation points in this book, but you're about to have three in a row, because Bats! Are! Great! Not only are they the only mammals that can fly (up to a hundred miles an hour, in the case of Mexican free-tailed bats), but their echolocation wizardry allows them to hunt in complete darkness.

Whichever grand deity runs the universe, She or He or They love them some bats, since worldwide there are at least fourteen hundred species. Some are as small as a quarter, and others have six-foot wingspans. They can be black, red, yellow, or white. Some are spotted, and some have striped faces. One kind in Borneo roosts inside the bell of pitcher plants; others nip the ribs of palm leaves to make the leaves collapse and form a protective tent. Some bats catch fish, others specialize in eating frogs, and a very few bats even make their living eating other bats.

Vampire bats do exist, but in Central and South America, not Transylvania. They are smaller than a goldfinch and weigh about an ounce—less than a shot of tequila. All vampires are obligate hematophages, which is to say, show a vampire the steaming haunch of a drowsy cow, and it will land nearby, creep close silently, make two surgical incisions, and lap up a few tablespoons

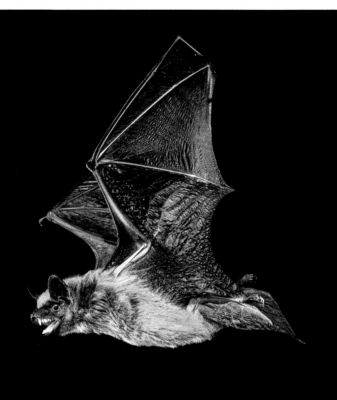

In color, size, and shape, this big brown bat is probably what most fossil bats looked like most of the time, going all the way back the Eocene.

of blood. They are not interested in people, and vampire bats do not want to get in your hair, roost in your attic, or crawl into the chicken coop and suck your brood hens dry.

Not just vampire bats make people nervy, but bats in general. Maybe it's because of our fear of the dark or maybe just random ignorance, but there is a lot of cultural prejudice against bats, such as the myth that all bats spread rabies. If you see a bat flopping around on the ground, don't pick it up. Otherwise, bats do not spread any more rabies than do infected dogs, cats, foxes, skunks, and raccoons.

Luckily, good information helps reverse fear. Merlin Tuttle is a researcher and conservationist who has done a lot of bat education. As he says, "It is simply amazing how quickly attitudes improve when people finally understand bats as they really are—sophisticated, beautiful, even cute, quite aside from their crucial roles as primary predators of insects, pollinators of flowers, and dispersers of seeds."

Go Two Stops Past Hand-Wing; Hang a Right at Echolocation

Bat evolution is interesting. The same question for them matches one for birds. How do you go from being a sort of proto-lemur (in the case of bats) to being a Top Gun aviator? It's not as though half a wing is that much use . . . or then again, maybe it is. Many animals glide tree to tree, from snakes in Borneo to Humboldt's flying squirrel in Yosemite. We are missing some of the fossils we wish we had for a full picture. To become a good fossil, make sure to die in a shallow lake, then be covered right away by a surge of anoxic mud or volcanic ash. If proto-bats were living in rain forests and scampering up and down trees, their chances of being preserved in a way that gives us fossil intermediaries would be dramatically reduced. Based on what information we have, it seems probable that bats went through a gliding stage before powered flight, but once they achieved flight, they began to look like modern bats right away.

However it got here, a bat's wing is just a supersized hand. The fingers have become stiff and long, but the bones match our own anatomy, with the addition of a tough membrane of skin stretched out between fingers. Bat wings can get holes in them, but even a tatty, beat-up wing still works. In fact, when you get a close-up view of a species that often catches prey on the ground, it can look like a B-17 that has come back from a particularly rough combat mission.

Echolocation evolved independently in two different bat lineages, as well as in unrelated groups such as rodents, cetaceans, and even a nocturnal bird, the oilbird from South America. To understand echolocation, first we need to remember that bats are not blind. Most bats have extremely good vision, with stereoscopic eyes adapted to help them find their way through the starlit night. Other bats, especially fruit-eating species, have keen senses of smell. And in the Americas, all bat species are excellent echolocators.

Echolocation is often compared to the *ping ping ping* of a submarine's sonar. The truth is more complicated than that. Bats use their mouths (oral echolocation) or noses (nasal echolocation) to create sounds that bounce off of objects. This gives them information about the distance from an object, and also its shape and even its composition.

Those sounds are for the most part undetectable for us. Humans have our best hearing from late teenage to young adulthood, perceiving sounds in the 20 to 20,000 Hertz ("Hz" and "kHz") range. In comparison to what we can hear, bat echolocation calls usually range from 15 kHz to 200 kHz. This means that some humans can hear some bats some of the time, but no human ears can hear all the bats all the time.

How quickly the echo returns tells the bat how far or near an object is. These probing "feeler" calls are emitted at different intervals depending on how often the bat needs to know where things are. A bat flying through an open field might emit sounds only once every second and sync that call with the wing beat to save energy. By contrast, a bat flying through the forest might emit calls several or even dozens of times per second, to microcorrect its flight path and avoid crashing into trees, vines, and leaves. That is a lot of signal being generated. How can bats navigate and hear only their own echoes in a cave when there are dozens, hundreds, or even hundreds of thousands of other bats flying at once?

Several solutions respond to these problems. We now know that bats have incredible sensitivity to changes in the frequency of sounds. Some bats can detect changes of 0.001 kHz, and they

This pallid bat has a hole in its wing yet still can keep flying. Many wild animals have dings and nicks.

can shift their own echolocation pitch higher or lower to differentiate theirs from that of other bats.

Bat calls are also incredibly loud—even if we cannot hear them ourselves. Bats emit sounds in the ultrasonic range up to 120 decibels, which in comparison is the same as what you would experience at a rock concert or trackside at a NASCAR race. Bats avoid being deafened by their own calls by partially disconnecting their ear bones with help of muscles that activate when the sounds are emitted, and then the bones reconnect to allow the bat to hear the echoes. This all happens multiple times per second, thousands of times in a single flight.

The shape of a bat's ears can also act as a filter, amplifying useful echoes and diminishing the less important ones.

The ghost-faced bat of Arizona and Texas looks as though it has its eyes inside its ears. To enhance hearing, the face is one giant reflecting dish.

This Mexican long-tongued bat uses low-volume echolocation calls that are difficult to pick up with bat detectors, unlike those of other North American species.

Many recent studies about bat echolocation involve their interactions with other species. A bat can emit calls that jam another bat's echolocation, to beat it to a prey item. Even more interesting, moths can detect approaching bats' calls and stop flying at the last moment to avoid being eaten. What makes this incredible is that moths are essentially deaf. They detect these calls because of vibrations inside their bodies. Moths are so good at avoiding bats that certain bat species have had to change their echolocation frequencies in order to have an advantage in this biological arms race.

Despite the fact that bat echolocation was discovered in the 1940s, we still have a lot to learn. One important aspect is that for most species, we don't know what their calls look like when transcribed by a bat detector's sonogram. That is because many bats emit sounds that are too weak to be picked up by even our best microphones. And because bats emit a range of calls depending on where they are navigating, the reference call recorded by a researcher releasing a captive bat might not match the sounds the animal would emit in a normal flight.

Slow Fliers versus Fast Fliers

There always is a trade-off between how fast versus how maneuverable airplanes, birds, and bats can be. Slower-flying bats have broad wings that create more lift at lower airspeeds. By contrast, the fighter jets of the bat world have narrow and pointy wings that need a lot more speed to create lift. A species such as the common vampire bat can take off easily from the ground due to its wing shape, and long-tongued bats can hover like hummingbirds when feeding. Neither, though, can shoot forward in a blur like the *Millennium Falcon* jumping into hyperspace. Other bats, such as Mexican free-tailed bats, can fly really fast, but need to roost on a cliff or cave ceiling so that they can achieve some momentum before getting airborne. Our largest free-tailed bat, the western mastiff bat (page 157), needs a twenty-foot drop in order to start flying.

These differences in flight have implications for other aspects of the bat's behavior. Fast fliers usually echolocate at lower frequencies because low-frequency calls can travel more distance, giving the bat more information on distant objects in open areas with time enough to correct their path. Slower bats echolocate at higher frequencies, since they need to "see" closer objects in the forest. Feeding strategy differs as well. Bats that fly in the open usually catch their prey during flight, while many forest dwellers glean, meaning they catch things on the ground or directly off vegetation.

Free-tailed bats like this mastiff bat have long, narrow wings optimized for high-speed, open-space flight. That comes at the expense of maneuverability.

Please Stand in This Bucket of Bleach Now: How We Study Bats

One can band bats the way one bands birds, and there are also miniature radio transmitters, but most study methods start with mist netting and having the bats "in the hand." Because a fungal disease called white nose syndrome is causing serious declines in colonial bat species, and because it can easily be spread by researchers going cave to cave, all equipment from boots to helmets needs to be stringently disinfected between sites.

Netting bats is similar to netting birds (page 134), other than it is done at night. Bats have varying personalities, the same as dogs or people. Some bats are cooperative when handled, even tame, while other individuals want very much to bite your thumb and all your fingers, and the thumbs and fingers of all your relatives and neighbors.

A handheld recorder or bat detector can let you detect bats around you by shifting the echolocation calls into ranges audible to humans. Not all bats emerge at the same times, so noting time of night can be an aid in identification. With bat calls, the idea of timed detection works passively; mount a detector on a pole or lash it to a tree, and if you have enough battery power, you can accumulate many weeks' worth of data. This system can work in cities as well; see page 192 to learn about Miguel Ordeñana's success in documenting urban bats.

Bats use caves, of course, but they also roost in palm trees, in old buildings, and under bridges. In the American West, the abundance of abandoned mines creates an abundance of good roost sites, but also an abundance of ways for humans to fall down a hole and die. Further, hibernating bats are vulnerable to disturbance, so managing agencies often weld bars across the mouths of adits, culverts, mine shafts, and natural caves. Bats can come and go freely, but vandals cannot.

top: Researchers stretch mist nets across a water hole in Arizona. They may capture ten different species before the night ends. **bottom:** This abandoned mine contains a bat colony. It is being gated for the bats' safety, and for the public's. **left:** A passive acoustic monitor in Arches National Park will record all the bats that echolocate in a fifty-meter radius.

A Bat Mini-Bestiary

Forty-four species of bat have been recorded in North America. The smallest is the canyon bat, and the largest is the western mastiff bat, which has a wingspan of just under two feet. In this photo pair, we see them side by side, printed to the same scale. (The mastiff is resting on a warm shoulder, since this injured bat was being rehabbed for release back into nature. Being so close to the handler made the bat feel secure.) Canyon bats are often the first bats out in the evening sky, while mastiff bats are so big you can see them—and hear their audible calls—even late at night. Unlike most other North American bats, mastiffs are active year-round.

To finish this chapter, we want to share with you five of our favorite bats.

The canyon bat is small, nimble, and often the first bat of the night.

The western mastiff bat is the largest bat in North America.

The spotted bat has the greatest ear-to-face ratio of any North American bat.

SPOTTED BAT

Spotted bats live throughout the West, and maybe they're rare, or maybe they're not—maybe we just are looking in the wrong places. Like the poorwill (page 125), spotted bats can enter torpor in cold weather. They eat moths and other aerial insects, tearing the wings off to chomp on the juicy main body. (Bat rehab folks feed a captive bat using tweezers and pet-store mealworms.) When they're in flight, you can identify spotted bats by their unique silhouette, and, with a spotlight, try to make out the black and white spots. If you are young and/or have great hearing, you may be able to pick out spotted bats as they hunt, since their calls just barely cross over into audible range. If you're male, or older, or you often listen to the car stereo cranked up high, then no, sorry, this species is going to be aurally invisible to you.

This hoary bat would almost make a good plush toy, but not quite.

HOARY BAT

Orange and black with a pug-like, smooshed-in face, the hoary bat is a mix of very beautiful and "Um, what kind of dog is *that*, anyway?" The common name references the salt-and-pepper fur that in some light looks like grass covered in hoarfrost. (It also looks like a desiccated leaf, which is good camouflage for a tree-roosting bat.) This is a widespread moth-eating species, usually solitary, that is found in many habitats. Like many bats, they are most active just after dark and then again before dawn, with a rest period in the middle of the night.

In the northern winter, hoary bats migrate south rather than hibernate, which may explain how they reached Hawaii. There they are called 'ōpe'ape'a, and they are now resident—they no longer try to commute back to the mainland. Over time, the Hawaiian form has evolved into its own species, as have some of the hoary bats in South America, which also have decided to stay put rather than migrate to and from North America.

TOWNSEND'S BIG-EARED BAT

If you're a birder, you know Townsend as a contemporary of John James Audubon, whose name is attached to a warbler, a shearwater, and a solitaire. Mammal spotters know Townsend's name from a mole, a vole, a chipmunk, and a ground squirrel, in addition to this large-eared bat. Alas, his name lived much longer than he did, since Townsend died young of arsenic poisoning, a common hazard for specimen-preparing, arsenic-using, nineteenth-century naturalists.

The bat itself is a real corker. Look at those ears! Obviously they help the bat hear well, but in deserts they may also dissipate heat, just the same way a jackrabbit's do. There is secondary evidence that the ears provide lift during flight.

Now one might assume that the Townsend's bat, with so much auditory acuity, would win every dogfight. But their target food, moths, have three ways of counteracting predation: they can try to jam bat echolocation; ordinary moths can generate the sound profile of distasteful ones; and moths can deflect sound waves to make their bodies appear smaller on the "radar screen" than they really are. Survival of the fittest, et cetera, and both sides have their offensive and defensive strategies.

Perhaps the name should be spelled with capital letters: Townsend's BIG-EARED bat.

MEXICAN FREE-TAILED BAT

This is a species that doesn't mind a crowd, and Bracken Cave in Texas has the world's largest bat colony, with twenty million Mexican free-tailed bats. In the evening, they pour out like smoke from a tanker fire. You also can see large emergences at Carlsbad Caverns National Park, at the Congress Avenue Bridge in Austin (page 193), and from the Yolo Bypass bridge on I-80 just east of Davis.

Some references call this the Brazilian free-tailed bat, based on the Latin name. No matter what it is called, this is a fast-flying, insect-munching bat, and it provides a service to farmers by eating crop pests before they become pests. They are good flyers; foraging, one bat might cover a hundred miles in a single night.

In winter this species migrates south, leaving the summering grounds in October and November. They'll be back soon, though; nursery colonies begin to form as early as February.

A Mexican free-tailed bat shows the "free" tail (not connected to flight membranes).

A group of pallid bats at a midnight roost in Arizona; they will disperse to hunt before dawn.

PALLID BAT

Another crowd favorite, the pallid bat is straw yellow and medium sized, and it eats scorpions, beetles, centipedes, crickets, and other arthropods that it gleans from branches or captures directly on the ground. It hunts a bit like a short-eared owl or northern harrier, flying slowly two to eight feet off the ground, with frequent dips, swoops, and glides. Expect it in rocky terrain, cliffs, and canyons, and from sea level up into the conifer belt.

Different species of bat come out at different stages of twilight. The pallid bat emerges late-ish, with an activity peak two hours after sunset, and a second activity burst shortly before dawn. To conserve energy, it undergoes shallow torpor daily. Rather than migrate, it hibernates near summer roosts.

Bats fill the skies at a popular bat-watching site near Davis.

Getting More Involved—Your First Bat Walk

Bat detectors are specialty tools and are priced as such, so unless you know somebody who has one, it's easiest to learn about bats on an organized night hike or bat walk.

To attend one, we recommend three approaches. The first is when you are in a major national park (Death Valley, Lava Beds, Carlsbad Caverns): check for the ranger talks that week. The

second is to be sure you know all the nonpark entities in your area, such as the Yolo Basin Foundation near Davis, California. They do bat events that include getting to meet animal ambassadors. Third, the website for Bat Conservation International has a tab on the left, "See Bats Live," and clicking that takes you to an interactive map of bat walks. We look forward to meeting you at an event soon.

"America for me has the pelt of a raccoon, / its eyes are the raccoon's black binoculars" —Czesław Miłosz

9

POCKET MICE
TO PUMAS
NOCTURNAL MAMMALS

The wolf exerts a powerful influence on the human
imagination. It takes your stare and turns it back on you.
—**Barry Lopez**

Worldwide there are about six thousand mammal species.
Many of these are poorly known (especially compared to birds),
so that total will surely become more refined in years to come.
New species will be discovered "hiding in plain sight" as one
general group is split into smaller units, and maybe all-new, previously unknown animals will be documented in an understudied forest or ocean. That a large percentage of the six thousand
total comes from the rodent groups should not negate the appeal
of the rest of the assemblage. After all, most birds are drab and
anonymous—proverbial "little brown jobs"—but that does not
lessen the impact of quetzals, macaws, or golden eagles. And
besides, at least in our view, deer mice and kangaroo rats are glorious in themselves.

Another significant percentage of the overall total comes
from the world's many bat species, and you already know how we
feel about those. We have not yet met the non-bat mammals, so
let's turn to those now.

Mesopredators, or How to Love Being the Middle Child

North America is home to a delicious assortment of midsized carnivores and omnivores, a faunal assemblage collectively called the mesopredators. Despite all the changes to the natural and built environments over the past hundred years, this group has managed to survive, perhaps because its members are good at inhabiting shadows and margins. This means that most of the "mesos" featured here occur in the *wild* wild, but also in or near the urban–wildland interface or even inside cities proper. For example, an estimated four thousand coyotes live in Chicago, and in Los Angeles, the death of P-22, Griffith Park's iconic mountain lion, resulted in tributes, poetry readings, and impromptu memorials citywide. Even badgers, normally considered an inhabitant of the wildest parts of the Wild West, can den on golf courses, presumably because the badgers are nocturnal while golfers are strictly diurnal.

Let's look at some of the interesting species you might encounter at night.

A coyote investigates a trail camera in Arizona.

Striped faced, sharp clawed, and busy digging a hole: must be a badger.

AMERICAN BADGER

Grizzle bodied and stripe faced, this low-to-the-ground power-house is the Lower 48's answer to the far north's wolverine.

Found from Canada to Mexico, American badgers prefer prairies and desert grasslands rather than forests; hunting in this open terrain, they dig out rodents, go after snakes and ground-nesting birds, and scavenge carrion. Although they generally live alone, badgers are still an essential member of a larger ecological community. Old badger dens are repurposed by kit foxes and burrowing owls, and at times coyotes follow badgers on their rounds, with the two species seemingly hunting in begrudging cooperation.

To see your first badger, the big parks are always a good bet: Point Reyes, Yellowstone, or the Carrizo Plains. That said, the iNaturalist map for American badger contains records from just about everywhere in the West, from Calgary to the Snake River in Idaho to the badlands of New Mexico. Good luck in your search, and when you find one, document it and post it, and that way you can help add a new square to the range map.

BOBCAT

A bobcat is a sandy brown (or blotchy gray) wildcat, bobtailed and rabbit focused. Its lanky legs make it seem bigger than its twenty pounds. It hunts on the ground with an ambushing pounce and a lethal bite to the victim's neck. While bobcats take a broad range of prey from quail to snakes, rabbits and jackrabbits are always the first choice.

Bobcats can occur in chaparral, desert scrub, mountain meadows—they are at home just about anywhere, even our urban edgelands. In California, bobcats live throughout the Bay Area, and there are photos of them napping on patio decks or hunting next to parked cars. The Seattle Urban Carnivore Project (hosted by the Woodland Park Zoo) uses camera traps and crowd-sourced reports to track bobcats—and also bears, coyotes, pumas, otters, and raccoons. Estimates in Phoenix list one bobcat per every two square miles. Further south, in Tucson, Sweetwater Wetlands (a marsh fed by treated wastewater) can have bobcats in the middle of the path in the middle of the day, especially in winter. Our twilight shot here was taken at Sweetwater.

To see if there are any bobcats near you, trail cameras can be fun to try. These use compact cameras and infrared flashes to document nighttime activity. The unit's housing is waterproof. You strap it to a tree or pole with a view of a likely animal pathway. You may be surprised to end up with a photograph like this one, which proved that bobcats were using a culvert behind a regular house in residential Los Angeles.

This bobcat is patrolling desert wetlands, but they can be found in almost all habitats, from high mountains to lowland scrub.

A trail camera captures a backyard bobcat.

COYOTE

Coyotes were originally native to the plains of the western half of the United States and Mexico, with at least a small presence as far south as Central America. (The name comes into English via Spanish, which adapted it from the Nahuatl word *coyōtl*.) It is tricky to reconstruct historical ranges since early observers often did not distinguish between coyotes and wolves, nor between wolves and the settlers' own fears and prejudices.

How nocturnal are coyotes? Completely so when they need to be. If you want to cross freeways or tip over trash cans, then it is best to hunt at night. The same if you want to catch opossums or climb into backyard fruit trees. The authors have seen and heard coyotes at night even in remote desert locations, so not just urban rhythms push them into the darkest hours. On average, though, if we magically were to remove all humans and all lighting from the equation, North America's coyotes would probably shift to being more diurnal than they are now.

In this plasticity of behavior, coyotes are good examples of opportunistic generalists. That includes what they are willing to consider a suitable dinner. Just to narrow down to one fifty-mile radius, in the San Francisco Bay Area coyotes have been known to eat apples, burritos, cats, crickets, dead seals and dead owls, fried chicken, jackrabbits, lizards, loquats, mice, pears, pigeons, pocket gophers, rabbits, rats, ravens, roadkill, scrub jays, snails, snakes, squirrels, and voles. They may or may not eat birdseed. (Are they after the seed or the mice the seed attracts?) Contrary to legend, if you hear a coyote pack yipping, it rarely means they are howling over a fresh kill. That would be a foolish thing to advertise— they do not want wolves or other coyotes coming to snatch away their just-caught dinner. *Yip yip* in solidarity, but never to gloat.

We should not have any coyotes left today, not if previous generations had been successful in their widespread persecution.

A golden sunrise makes this well-fed coyote look even more light-blessed than usual.

Yet a map of North America and a map of the range of *Canis latrans* now overlap in a perfect Venn diagram. Two centuries of hunting, trapping, poisoning, and disinheriting have not driven coyotes to extinction. If anything, since we got rid of wolves, coyotes have enjoyed being able to expand into more niches and to do so with less competition. They are thriving, both despite and because of us.

What about the future? It is easy to be optimistic. To quote the poet Charles Wright, "Coyotes, cockroaches, and the sonnet will always be with us."

A camera trap's flash captures a gray fox in the snow.

GRAY FOX

Gray foxes look very foxy: alert ears, low body, bushy tail. Yet the common name undersells this handsome beast, whose gray body is really a rich mix of silver and black, complemented by a blaze of white and cinnamon. Red foxes have white-tipped tails; gray foxes, by contrast, have black tail tips. A coyote looks taller, rangier, and more jackal faced than a gray fox, and a kit fox is smaller and paler, and is more often found in open, desert habitat.

Gray foxes give complex vocalizations. Besides regular barking and yipping, these foxes, as naturalists studying Chesapeake Bay have pointed out, "have also been known to growl, snarl, squeal, screech, and chuckle." It and the closely related island fox are unique in another way: they can climb trees, something other canids cannot easily do.

They are widespread and easy to find. Charles remembers the first gray fox he ever saw. He was backpacking at Point Reyes with his high school biology class, and one night a fox ran through the campsite. If you want to jump-start your fox count, just go to Point Reyes National Seashore and drive park roads at night. They also are seen around nearby towns, such as Olema and Point Reyes Station.

Bandit mask and striped tail help identify the ubiquitous raccoon.

RACCOON

Raccoons have big butts and a sort of waddling gait, but they can run quickly; and with their nimble paws, they can lock-pick their way into trash bins, compost sheds, and any outbuilding with a sign that says Raccoons Keep Out. Even biologists who should know better call them trash pandas, but instead of mocking them, we might pause to admire how a stream-and-wetland species like the raccoon has managed to navigate culverts and storm drains to establish colonies in desert towns far from the nearest water.

All raccoons have a grizzled gray body and striped tail, with said tail being the distinguishing feature of the "coon-skin cap" popular in America since colonial times. Mountain lions eat raccoons, as do great horned owls, and alligators and pythons in Florida. A fully grown raccoon can usually fend off an attacking coyote and, less often, a bobcat. We are their single biggest predator: each year, millions end up as gray lumps on the side of the road, hit by speeding cars. Even liberal California has a raccoon-hunting season, and here is where we use our sarcastic voice: *Really?* Can't we just let nature alone for once?

At the same time, there are almost certainly more raccoons now than at any time since the start of the European conquest, and we can't think of a single American city that doesn't have raccoons somewhere in it or very nearby. Although the amount of roadkill is depressing, it also is a way of reminding us how many more animals are out there, unseen and uncounted.

SKUNK

We should say "skunks," plural, since in North America there are five species: striped, hooded, hog-nosed, western spotted, and eastern spotted. Most common of the five is the striped skunk, the kind shown here. Poor eyesight but good aim means it bumbles along looking for insects or fallen fruit, unconcerned about what's nearby. If you are standing still, even if you are taking flash photographs, it often ignores you, though if it spins and lifts its tail, back off quickly.

This is one of the lighter animals in this section, with a typical adult weighing more than a cat but less than a corgi, and it is just the right size to be taken by great horned owls (who have no sense of smell). Other predators such as coyotes do not want to mess with it: nobody can afford to lose stealth by being saturated with stink juice for a week or longer. Would a just-sprayed animal also have trouble tracking prey, if the skunk smell overpowers their ability to distinguish other scents? The authors are not sure, but assume so.

Name origin goes back to Algonquin and more or less means "pee fox." Raise your hand if you think we should start using that phrase today.

Black-and-white markings and a feather duster tail can only mean one animal: striped skunk.

Nature may be "red in tooth and claw," but it has many vegetarians, too. Let's honor them as well.

WOOD RATS

These are also called pack rats, and their nests can be gigantic. The animals themselves are large (as mouse-sized creatures go), and in North America there are a dozen species, mostly separated by range. (On the ground, they all look more or less the same.) Large eyes and radar-dish ears help it forage in the dark. Wood rats eat seeds and cactus fruit, and meet most of their water needs that way too. The really great thing about them is the nests, which are also called debris piles or middens; in the Southwest, some of these are thousands of years old. They last so long because of the arid climate, by being protected in rock alcoves of cliffs and caves, and by being coated in a varnish of crystallized urine. These middens can provide a detailed record of climate change, almost like the strata of an archaeological dig. According to the National Park Service, "Because pack rats carried bits of pottery, twine, and other artifacts from nearby human settlements into their shelters, the stratified middens also capture cultural history at a point in climatic time. Radiocarbon dating of the pack rats' middens enables scientists to create a chronology for the relationships between people, deforestation and resource depletion, and climatic changes."

That's pretty cool for a pile of sticks and ancient pee-pee. As a side note, these animals like shiny things, so if you can't find your car keys, maybe a wood rat took them.

A desert wood rat tells the photographer, "I see you!"

Six-foot-tall hiker for scale, so you can see how tall and wide this wood rat nest is.
Studying it can reveal climate data going back hundreds, even thousands, of years.

KANGAROO RAT

The biologist's nickname for this group is "k-rat," usually uttered with tender affection. Most species look like the Merriam's kangaroo rat shown here, with big eyes; a round body; a long, tuft-tipped tail; and a blond-and-white color pattern. They do not need to drink water, getting that from their food. These are well named (or at least the "kangaroo" part applies well), since powerful hind legs allow it to outjump even a striking rattlesnake, with the world record being nine feet in a single leap.

Although k-rats live in chaparral, they are easier to see in—and most commonly associated with—deserts, especially Death Valley and Joshua Tree National Parks.

All kangaroo rats are nocturnal (hence the large eyes), yet they also can see a range of light that humans cannot, since their vision extends into the ultraviolet spectrum. This was only recently confirmed. Question now is, Why? Possible answers include enhanced seed-spotting capability, as an aid in navigation underground and at twilight, being able to see other rodents' pee, or just a vestigial skill they inherited from an ur-gopher ancestor twenty-five million years ago and never lost.

A kangaroo rat can see wavelengths of light that we cannot.

A cottontail warily studies the photographer.

RABBITS AND HARES

Rabbits are rabbits, and a jackrabbit is a bigger kind of rabbit called a hare. On back roads in open country, these are the most commonly encountered nighttime animals. Hares and rabbits share similar characteristics, including the ears-and-cotton-tail body plan. Tall, thin ears dissipate heat and focus sound; short, thick ears conserve heat. This means that if you see a photo of a rabbit, even a species new to you (such as the wooly hare of Tibet), you can look at the ears and guess its likely habitat.

Rabbits and cars, oh what a sad dance that can become. When a predator approaches, rabbits rely on camouflage and staying still right up until the last minute, then they sprint away. They are definitely not used to handling the dangers of cars and trucks, which have a mesmerizing headlight beam and a velocity far beyond anything a rabbit was ever programmed to understand.

That is why if you're driving on a dirt road at night in the desert, and if there's a desert cottontail within twenty meters of the edge of the road, no matter which way it is headed or how cautiously you try to drive, there is a 100 percent chance that the rabbit is going to come up to the edge of the road, wait until just the last moment, and then dash in front of your car. We talk about something being drawn to an object like a moth to a flame, but the idiom might be better updated to be "drawn like a rabbit to headlights."

When not patrolling nocturnal roads, rabbits do what they have always done: they hop, they eat, they make more rabbits. All of North America's rabbits and hares (about a dozen species total) are the foundational prey everything else relies on.

MULE DEER

You already know this animal, and perhaps even see it daily in your yard or when driving to work. If you have been to Sequoia or Yosemite, you've seen it there too. This means you know that deer can be diurnal (out in the daytime), but also crepuscular

This deer has bedded down in a nest of chicken wire and grass, yet other mule deer forage all night.

(out at dusk). And while some deer bed down at night in a thicket or tall grass, both authors can attest that in our nighttime travels, there are a lot of deer out then too, and sometimes even in neighborhoods that are seemingly deer-free during the day.

What makes some deer come out only at night? When hunting season starts, that can partially explain it, since bucks soon learn to avoid high-visibility times of the day. But even in non-hunting areas, some mule deer are nocturnal and others are not. Why? If you know the answer, write to us care of the publisher. Our own theories include the quality of forage (perhaps they need to feed longer in some areas, so can't bed down) or how likely or unlikely a nighttime ambush by a mountain lion might be. In some areas, it may be safe to hunker down and not risk making noise by walking around.

Or maybe most deer are active both during the day (for part of the day) and at night (for part of the night), and our cultural bias toward demarcating "work" from "play" from "sleep" means that we struggle to understand the more flexible stop-and-start rhythms of our fellow mammals.

And at the Apex . . .

We can't leave out the mega-megas, the tippy top of the trophic pyramid, the animals we all want to see (though maybe from the car, not in the middle of the trail).

BLACK BEAR

Black bears in North America are always bears, but only sometimes black. That is because black bears can also be brown, cinnamon, tan, and spirit blue. Males weigh more than females, and both weigh more in fall, pre-hibernation, than they will in spring. Despite extravagant claims and the occasional outlier, they're smaller than you might guess—in the West, about an average of 250 pounds.

Zoo bears weigh more than wild bears, and the once-every-hundred-years kinds of black bears (usually shot by hunters back east) can reach seven hundred pounds. Charles once helped carry a sedated black bear in Sequoia (a problem bear that was going to be relocated), and even though it was only a small-to-medium one, it was still more than he and the ranger wanted to carry very far. A two-hundred-pound bear weighs much more than that in the dark, especially when you know there are other, unsedated bears all around you.

As with coyotes, bears might naturally be a mix of diurnal and crepuscular by default, but they are now nocturnal either to avoid humans or to access food that humans control. And bears may forage at night to fatten up for hibernation; or, just due to a quirk of personality, that is what they most feel like doing. It can be risky to be a bear at night, though, since an average of twenty bears a year are hit by cars in Yosemite National Park, mostly after dark.

Black bears famously eat everything from acorns to ants, carp to carrion, pine cones to picnic baskets. If they smell food inside a vehicle and decide they want to investigate it, they can pry open a car door as easily as somebody opening a can of Diet Coke.

This bear wants in *so bad*, but modern park dumpsters are bear proof. This is good for us and for them.

A motorcycle passed, and during the night, so did a black bear.

Anytime a bear wins at the food game, it will only try harder next time. This harms the bears long term, since as the bumper stickers warn us, "A fed bear is a dead bear."

MOUNTAIN LION (OR PUMA)

They're *baaaack*. Although still hunted in most states, mountain lions have recovered to near-historical levels, or maybe-probably-we-wish-upon-a-star they have. They sure can be hard to census. Trackers look at scat and footprints, other researchers tally kill sites or catch them in baited traps to put on radio collars, and we can collect roadkilled pumas from freeway berms and analyze security camera footage, and with all the data, come up with population numbers that we hope are at least approximately correct.

And the general consensus is that they're back.

We know their basic biology at least. They are generally but not consistently nocturnal, since it's easier to stalk prey with darkness on your side. An adult mountain lion kills and eats about one deer per week, with about a 50 percent success rate when hunting. They also eat nondeer creatures, so one mountain

It's a big brown cat with a long tail, and that means "puma."

lion became a specialist in killing badgers, while another one in Nevada mostly went after mustangs. The Griffith Park cat, P-22, once ate a koala from the zoo and a Chihuahua on a leash, though that was at the end of its life, when it was old and ill. In California, one might wish pumas could take out more feral pigs than they do, to help control these destructive, nonnative porcines, but the two don't have ranges that overlap all that often. And if we could negotiate with pumas, we might ask them to go easy on the bighorn sheep, since those populations remain small and vulnerable. But a puma's gotta do what a puma's gotta do, so prey is prey, endangered or not.

The one group that should not worry is humans, since you're a thousand times more likely to get hit by lightning than to be

A deer mouse waits on a researcher's glove, ready to be ID'd.

attacked by a mountain lion (and ten thousand times more likely to die in a car accident than you are to be the victim of a lightning strike). Usual advice still applies: if you see a mountain lion on the trail, be loud and proud, and whatever you do, don't crouch down and try to scuttle away while making little mewing sounds.

The good news is that if you hike enough miles in the right habitat, you're bound to see one eventually, which most of us covet doing. Between here and there, another cliché is also true: lots more mountain lions saw you before you saw them.

Getting More Involved—How to Identify Nocturnal Rodents

Many birdwatchers keep lists of the birds they have seen. Less known but equally satisfying: tracking one's mammal species, from orcas to orangutans. And this means that for a full list, mice matter too. Even if you're not quite that dedicated, it's fun to know what's around.

Professionals trap rodents for study in a metal box called a Sherman trap, baiting it with oatmeal and peanut butter. Modern cameras produce photographs so good that you can see things previously only visible when the animal was "in hand"; one picture is worth a thousand words or two or three Sherman traps. Morbid to admit, but roadkill is another way to survey local possibilities; both José and Charles currently have deceased kangaroo rats and window-strike birds bagged and labeled in their freezers, awaiting transfer to the appropriate museum. (The trick is to remember to warn visiting houseguests.)

Fiona Reid's *Mammals of North America* remains our top pick for a field guide, though Heyday's *Californian's Guide to the Mammals among Us* works well too. Despite "California" in the title, half the photographs were taken in Washington, Oregon, Nevada, Arizona, or New Mexico, including the deer on the cover. (*Shhh*—don't tell anybody.)

José prepares to photograph a deer mouse in the California desert.

"Los Angeles looks like Hell with a good electrician."
—apocryphal quotation from an unnamed screenwriter

10

TOWNS AND CITIES
AFTER DARK

I loved P-22 and hold a deep respect for his intrepid spirit, charm, and just plain chutzpah. We may never see another mountain lion stroll down Sunset Boulevard or surprise customers outside the Los Feliz Trader Joe's. But perhaps that doesn't matter—what matters is P-22 showed us it's possible. —**Beth Pratt, National Wildlife Federation**

Cities ≠ nature—or so we've been led to believe. Yet from the leopards of Mumbai to the "townie" bears of South Lake Tahoe, we live in a world where it is increasingly hard to say where nature stops and urbania begins. For example, there are the thousands of coyotes that live in Chicago and San Francisco and other major cities. To them they are "in" nature, or in as much nature as they are ever likely to know. No coyote wakes up and thinks, "Shoot dang, I am not a real, authentic animal because I decided to live in Seattle." In the hills around Los Angeles, researchers have documented over one hundred different mountain lions since studies began in 2002. The most famous of these was P-22, the puma who sometimes left Griffith Park and went for a stroll along the sidewalks of residential Silver Lake—though only in the middle of the night, never daylight. "The city at three a.m. is an ungodly mask / the approaching day hides behind," the poet Yusef Komunyakaa writes. He adds, "hides behind / and from."

That mask is worn by a lot of animals, all in all. We met the mesopredators in the previous chapter—skunks, bobcats, raccoons—but it turns out even bats manage to thrive in urban areas. Our consideration of nature in the nighttime city will start with them.

Bridges (Are the New Bat Houses)

One fabulous public bat-watching spot is not in a national park but adjacent to the Congress Avenue Bridge in Austin, Texas. Mexican free-tailed bats roost under the bridge and emerge at dusk to feed across the surrounding countryside. The size of the emergence varies daily, but the total size of the colony is 1.5 million bats, so some summer nights the bats come out, and come out, and come out—an infinite stream of bats seems to be flowing out from under the bridge and rising over the Colorado River. You can watch the emergence from the banks on each side, from on top of the bridge itself, or from charter boats idling below in the water. (Note: this is a different "Colorado" than the river that flows through Moab and the Grand Canyon.) It's a grand social spectacle, so come to watch the bats, but stay to watch the people. Austin's abundance of good food and good music only adds to the appeal.

Los Angeles has multiple bat species too, as we know thanks to the work of Miguel Ordeñana from the Natural History Museum of Los Angeles County. It was his "intended-for-bobcats" camera trap that first discovered the existence of Puma 22 in Hollywood. In a different and more ambitious project, Miguel has been putting up passive bat recording stations all over the city, from public parks to private backyards, and documenting the species that pass by each location.

He has found that Los Angeles has hosted nineteen species of bats. That total includes some of the types covered earlier in this book (hoary bat, canyon bat, and western mastiff bat), plus

This photo captures an emergence of just a few of the 1.5 million Mexican free-tailed bats that live under the Congress Avenue Bridge in Austin, Texas.

bats that add even more colors to the chart—the western red bat, western yellow bat, and silver-haired bat. The bat called Yuma myotis likes to hunt over water, so can be expected along the Los Angeles River or even the Wilshire Boulevard. pond at the La Brea Tar Pits. The big brown bat (page 146) occurs in Southern California as well, as does the pocketed free-tailed bat, found here at the northern edge of its range.

How can this all be? In the popular imagination, all cities may be bad, but Los Angeles is the baddest bad place of all. Everybody knows it is nothing more than a concrete jungle— Axl Rose even said so, on the album *Appetite for Destruction*. Yet everywhere Miguel Ordeñana has put up bat detectors, even in the least promising, most built-up sites, he has gotten hits. The number of bats migrating through, summering in, and roosting

Miguel Ordeñana checks the memory card on a pole-mounted bat detector in a community park.

around Los Angeles County shows how hollow all these "wasteland" clichés are, and reminds us once again that until somebody has actively looked, we can't assume that any given piece of the planet, no matter how urbanized, contains nil nature.

Who Else Likes Cities?

Who likes cities? Snowy owls would be one possible answer, or at least the immature snowy owl that decided to roost on rooftops in Orange County, California, in the winter of 2022–23. It probably arrived in Southern California on a cargo ship, but once here, it could be seen next to chimneys and air vents in the most residential of residential neighborhoods. Thousands of people came to see it.

Or answer two, spiders. Spiders need a place to put up a web, and they need prey items. After that, tree or parking structure, state park or derelict barn, it's all the same to them. A vacant lot can be a pennant festival of plastic bags waving over a shining sea of broken glass, but so long as there are things to eat and so long

This immature snowy owl wintered on a roof in Orange County, delighting thousands.

An orb weaver spider wraps prey in downtown Los Angeles.

A baby javelina crosses a rain-wet parking lot.

as its web is not walked into too many times per day, no spider in the world is going to say, *But it's so ugly.*

If you love salamanders, move to Portland, Oregon, since inside the city limits you can find over twenty kinds of amphibians, from newts to tree frogs. A bit to the north, Seattle's Puget Sound garter snake is slate gray with turquoise stripes. You never know what you'll find if you are open to experience. In Portland, in the botanical gardens, Charles saw his "lifer" mountain beaver. (If you keep a list of animals, every added species is a special thrill: glory be to each new entry.) Also called aplodontia, this is an odd, rarely seen animal, chunky and tailless, the only representative of its genus and family. It is a relic from earlier times: despite the name, aplodontia is not a beaver, but instead a primitive rodent. When Charles saw one, there was no warning, no posts on the mammal-watching sites—he was looking for salamanders in a botanical garden and found an utterly fabulous black hamster instead. Luckily for him, this animal didn't know it wasn't supposed to live in a city.

Or in another example, in residential Tucson, javelinas (relatives of wild pigs, also called peccaries) have adapted to urban life. Once the sun goes down, they casually cross streets, graze lawns, or trot with their young past sports cars in upscale developments. They may even rest during the heat of the day under mobile homes. Javelina herds are called sounders, and some sounders number up to fifty animals, although ten is more typical. It can be fun (and nearly alarming) to see a gang of a dozen javelinas taking over an apartment's public spaces.

Mountain lions stalk javelinas in the adjacent canyons and mountains, but they typically do not enter into the "streetlight zone" of suburban Tucson. Javelinas thus gain protection by hanging out near town, and also gain additional sources of food.

And here is a "foxier" example. As habitat for the San Joaquin kit fox was lost to oil wells and monocrop agriculture, and as coyotes and nonnative red foxes predated them or competed for

This kit fox pup waits for its parents to return. The adults have made an abandoned house their new den.

An urban javelina auditions for its close-up.

A great horned owl scowls from the roof of a college library, Lancaster, California.

food and den sites, things began to look grim—so bad for the fox that in 1967 it was listed as endangered. And then the foxes surprised us. Bakersfield became "kit fox central," with a population that reached a high count of five hundred foxes. The foxes found ways to navigate the city using culverts and storm drains and power line rights-of-way—they existed in edges and shadows, as we have seen before—and meanwhile, the local human residents, better informed than they had been in years previous, did their best to coexist.

The rose-ringed parakeet also has recently made a home in urban Bakersfield, though unlike the foxes, these lime-green parrots are not native, so they contribute more to aesthetics than to ecological diversity.

The final example is the great horned owl. If you take a record aggregator such as iNaturalist and look at the sighting map for great horned owl, an interesting pattern emerges. In any of the big cities of the West—Phoenix, Reno, San Francisco, Sacramento, Portland—the density of owl records increases inside the city circle as compared to the landscape around it.

Most of that reporting reflects observer bias. People live and work and commute in cities, and they post what they see, which will mostly be wildlife in cities. Yet the quantity of reports also reflects quality (or at least variety) of habitat. Cities have cemeteries, rights-of-way, nice houses with big yards and tall landscaping. Cities have rats and park squirrels and skunks and stray cats. Cities do not have hunting or little kids shooting pellet guns. Cities are therefore potentially good places to be an owl.

Light Pollution—Problems and Solutions

Cities are bright places—often too bright. They don't need to be, and some people are working to change things for the better. It's not that it is wrong to want a light over your door or for a school crossing in the morning; it's a matter of *how* things are lit, and by what kinds of fixtures.

Similar to forests and other habitats, dark skies—those skies that are visually intact and not whitewashed with the slushy luminance of human lighting—are also environments that can become endangered. Light pollution increases with urbanization and creates zones where only the brightest of the stars can be seen.

Besides denying us our visual heritage, light pollution affects wildlife movement and behavior patterns. Migrating birds fly into buildings, insects circle porch lights until exhausted (or until they are eaten by a bat), and flower blooms arrive at the wrong time (or not at all). Swedish bat biologist Johan Eklöf: "In England, researchers have studied meadows in Cornwall, in particular the

In this community, houses have telescopes, not streetlights.

bird's-foot trefoil," a heath plant with yellow flowers. Normally, they attract large numbers of aphids, but when street lights alter circadian rhythms, the "absence of flowering can decimate entire populations of aphids, which in turn affects green lacewings, damselflies, ladybirds, [and] hoverflies." He speaks of this collapse as creating "disorder in the system."

Most of this pollution comes from "light spills." Aim street lights down, not up; and in offices, if people are not working, turn the lights off entirely. In addition to saving energy, dark-sky policies grant citizens a better connection to the night sky. The International Dark-Sky Association spearheads these policies and also directs people to community science projects where they can help out.

One of these projects is a basic test to see where the darkness is and isn't. As you would when doing a breeding bird survey, you go out and check the status of your local sky. There are dates each month when you would do this observation, to make the results quantifiable; there are also guidelines for measuring and reporting, using a modified version of the Bortle scale we met earlier. The program is called Globe at Night and is under the auspices of the National Science Foundation; it allows community scientists to contribute information about night-sky brightness to our general astronomical knowledge. One designated week a month, everyone is invited to go outside more than an hour after sunset (8 to 10 p.m., local time) to look for one common constellation designated by the association. After your eyes adjust to the dark, use a star map or night-sky app to find the constellation in question and observe how many stars you can see: Just the main ones of the core constellation? Or many more points of light? Was it a cloudy or clear night? Then go to the website (https://www.globeatnight.org/webapp/) to report your observations and contribute to our understanding of light pollution's impact.

Just because a lot of people live in one place, cities do not have to be so bright that you can see them from outer space. You can limit billboards and still have viable commerce; and on the billboards you do have, you can light them in a way that doesn't waste light or electricity. Flagstaff in northern Arizona was the first "dark-sky city" in the world. This was greatly influenced by the existence of many observatories in the area, the most famous being the Lowell Observatory, where Pluto was first discovered. Flagstaff's choices could be models for others.

Some smaller communities have opted to be entirely dark: no streetlights at all. In Sky Village near the Chiricahua Mountains of Arizona, all the houses were built in a way that keeps the night sky pristine. According to the sales listings, residents who move there can become "part of an astronomy community committed to dark skies, the continued exploration of the night sky through

The Milky Way rises above Flagstaff, Arizona.

astrophotography, visual observing, and astronomy education." Such people might agree with Johan Eklöf: "Seize darkness. Become its friend and enjoy it—it will enrich your life."

What Comes Next?

For better or worse, we live in a time of paradox and opportunity. This means that the following statements are equally true: mankind has ruined nature; mankind will be saved by nature; nature is so big and complex and resilient, we couldn't kill nature if we tried our darnedest; if we do ever kill it, then all right, nature is dead—and long live nature, since it will come right back, as strange and glorious and powerful as ever.

Our final image in this chapter is about faith and hope, which is to say, it is about the future. In Southwestern tradition, December nights include one or more Noches de Luminarias, nights when lit candles mark processionary paths to a church or plaza. We end with a luminaria pathway at Tumacácori, a mission in southern Arizona now preserved as a historical park.

The National Park Service manages the site, and its website sketches the region's dense history. "Tumacácori," the site explains, "sits at a cultural crossroads in the Santa Cruz River valley. Here O'odham, Yaqui, and Apache people met and mingled with European Jesuit and Franciscan missionaries, settlers, and soldiers—sometimes in conflict and sometimes in cooperation."

Night for us includes bears and coral snakes and feeder-raiding nectar bats. But night includes the human experiences as well—the simple pleasures of making tacos at the trailhead, or the stories we tell ourselves about starlight, about where it came from and what it means now that it has gotten here. Night for us is friendship and laughter, wet shoes and dropped cameras. And it is also knowledge and passion, investigation and faith. Mankind will go back to the Moon almost certainly, and to more distant places after that. Here on Earth, we will rediscover long-lost nightjars or even come across mammals completely new to science. There will always be new bats to photograph and new parks to visit, and that is a good thing, a hopeful thing.

Past those facts and achievements, the largest truth about nature at night is that night is a place of infinite wonder. If you stretch out under a ponderosa pine as Georgia O'Keefe did, you get to experience the shape (and vanilla smell) of the tree, the warmth of the ground under you, and the sound of the great horned owl a few trees over. But you also can allow yourself to look past the branches up into a sky of immense size and ageless beauty. You just have to give the night a few moments of calm, uninterrupted presence and the starlight will pour into you, no tools or training required.

The tree, the ground, the owl, the sky, the art and the stories that the art tells—such great gifts these all are, such an infinite blessing of hope and possibility.

These have been our experiences at night, anyway, and we hope they will be yours, too.

Lit candles called luminaria mark Christmas Eve at Tumacácori, a former mission.

IMAGE CREDITS

The authors thank the following individuals and organizations for their photographs included in this book (page number follows credit):

S. Anderson (National Park Service), 92

Andrew Cattoir (National Park Service), 22, 46–47

René Clark (Dancing Snake Nature Photography), 66, 73, 80–81, 83 (bottom), 86, 93, 113, 122

Gavin Emmons (National Park Service), 114

Salle Engelhardt (National Park Service), 117

Jacob W. Frank (National Park Service), 27

Seth Goodspeed (National Park Service), 169

John Haubrich, 171 (bottom)

Fred Hood, viii, 55, 57, 62, 94, 106, 120, 166, 171 (top), 175, 196 (bottom), 199, 206–7

NASA, 41

National Park Service (uncredited), 52, 105, 116, 155 (lower right), 158

Jim Peaco (National Park Service), 127, 185

William Pedro (National Park Service), ii

Tim Rains (National Park Service), 130–31

Scott Rheam (USFWS), 15

Matthias Süßen (Creative Commons Attribution-Share Alike 4.0 license), 39

Waldemar Manfred Seehagen (Shutterstock), 187

Veronica Verdin (National Park Service), 155 (lower left)

Alun Williams333 (Creative Commons Attribution-Share Alike 4.0 license), 112

Andrea Willingham (National Park Service), 115

Jeff Zylland (National Park Service), 43

Special thanks to the following organizations for use of paintings in the book:
page 7
Georges Trubert (French, active 1469–1508)
The Annunciation to the Shepherds
Tempera colors, gold leaf, gold and silver paint, ink
J. Paul Getty Museum, Ms. 48 (93.ML.6), fol. 54v

page 21
Georgia O'Keeffe (American, 1887–1986)
The Lawrence Tree, 1929
Oil on canvas, 31 x 40 in. (78.7 x 101.6 cm)
Wadsworth Atheneum Museum of Art, Hartford, CT
The Ella Gallup Sumner and Mary Catlin Sumner Collection Fund, 1981.23

The aurora borealis is usually only seen in the far north, including this view from a ship in the North Sea. But they are part of the West, and in 2023 a giant solar flare made the northern lights visible as far south as Ogden, Utah, and Mammoth Mountain in California.

In the American West, large fires are part of the new nightscape, whether we like it or not. Always follow evacuation orders, as the authors are doing here.

ABOUT THE AUTHORS

Poet and naturalist **Charles Hood** lives in the Mojave Desert. He recently released two books with Heyday: *Wild Sonoma* and *A Salad Only the Devil Would Eat: The Joys of Ugly Nature.* While working on this book, Charles passed the thousand-species mark on his world mammal list—an achievement that he says "ranks somewhere between being a local pickleball champion and accumulating the world's largest ball of string." Always ready for the next excursion, he owns three bat detectors, nine headlamps and flashlights, and a hard-copy world atlas, "since you never know when Siri will go wonky on you."

José Gabriel Martínez-Fonseca divides his time between Nicaragua and Arizona, where he recently completed a PhD in bat ecology. He owns almost as many headlamps and cameras as Charles does and has contributed images to wildlife publications worldwide. He is also very adroit at catching specimens, including the tarantula he is holding here (featured also on page 71). José is the coauthor, along with Charles Hood and Erin Westeen, of *Sea Turtles to Sidewinders: A Guide to the Most Fascinating Reptiles and Amphibians of the West.*